TOOLS OF THE TRADE FOR CANADIAN G~~ENE~~~~ALOG~~Y

A GUIDE FOR ~~CANADI~~ANS RESEARCH~~ING IN~~ CANADA

revised and expanded

Althea Douglas M.A. C.G. (C.)

The Ontario Genealogical Society
2004

© 2004 The Ontario Genealogical Society and Althea Douglas
All rights reserved. No part of this publication may be reproduced, stored
in a retrieval system or transmitted in any form or by any means — electronic, mechanical, photocopying, microreproduction, recording or oth-
erwise — without prior written permission of the publisher.

Further copies of this book and information about the Society can be
obtained by writing to:
The Ontario Genealogical Society
Suite 102, 40 Orchard View Boulevard
Toronto ON M4R 1B9
Canada

National Library of Canada Cataloguing in Publication
Douglas, Althea, 1926-
  Tools of the trade for Canadian genealogy : a guide for family
historians researching in Canada / Althea Douglas. — Rev. and
expanded

Includes bibliographical references and index.
ISBN 0-7779-2134-0
  1. Canada—Genealogy—Handbooks, manuals, etc. I. Ontario
Genealogical Society. II. Title.

CS82.D683 2004   929'.1'072071   C2003-906417-4

Cover designed by Digital Chaos
Printed by Hume Imaging

Published by The Ontario Genealogical Society
Suite 102, 40 Orchard View Boulevard
Toronto ON M4R 1B9
Canada
416-489-0734
provoffice@ogs.on.ca
www.ogs.on.ca

Published with assistance from the Ontario Ministry of Culture

Contents

Introduction

I am a researcher
You are a librarian
He is an archivist
We are genealogists

When I put together *Here Be Dragons* from a collection of explanatory sheets I wrote for clients and some magazine articles, it was meant to fill in some of the gaps in researchers' historical knowledge of Canada. As I meet people climbing their family tree, both beginners and those who have been *doing* their families for years, I have become aware of gaps in some people's research background. Again, it is mostly a matter of things "everyone" knows and so never pass on to those who don't.

Tools of the Trade for Canadian Genealogy is a collection of essays relating to archives, records and ways to approach family research in Canada, for both those who live here and those whose family moved through on their way to greener pastures. Its purpose is to start the researcher thinking about why information survives or is destroyed, who kept records, why they were kept and where they may have ended up, as well as in what form you may access them today.

Whatever I write will eventually be wrong, but that is nothing new. In my lifetime the nature of research has moved from hand-written copies of original records assembled in Ottawa, to microforms of rare books and manuscripts available through inter-library loans, to digitized documents accessible on-line in your own home.

Today's computerized catalogues and searchable databases mean that libraries, archives and museums now make their holdings accessible to users in similar ways. However, it is important to realize these various types of repositories assembled their holdings under very different mandates and philosophies. Understanding where archives, libraries and museums have come from will make it easier for searchers to figure out where to find what they want.

The Catch-22 of genealogy is that to find tax rolls, church registers, newspapers or cemeteries, you must know where your ancestor lived. Some of the massive indexes and databases we can now access make locating our ancestors much simpler, and a discussion of what is out there and how to make the best use of it comes with a warning. Although we are grateful for these tools that devoted workers have produced, perhaps our gratitude blinds us to some of the errors and omissions that make some of these tools suspect. Use the latest tools, but always check the original sources.

Once our ancestors are fixed in time and place, there are ways of finding out more about them and the lives they lived. Official name lists — be they tax rolls, census records, or militia lists — confirm residence; cemetery inscriptions and burial registers lead to obituaries in newspapers, and the local papers tell many stories to enliven a family history. Maps and geography explain many things.

Parts of these articles have been published before, but all have been revised and updated. The ever-increasing quantity of material now available, both electronically and in print — particularly indexes to census returns and newspapers — makes it impossible to compile "complete" lists. By the time they are in print, they are obsolete. Instead, I have tried to suggest where and how to look for the latest information on what is available. I hope some of these suggestions will help you find your way back into the lives your ancestors lived.

My thanks to the staff at the reference room desks of the Library and Archives of Canada for their unfailing help and cooperation as I found my way through the wealth of material they hold. As always, I appreciate proofreading help by my husband and the encouragement and assistance of the Ontario Genealogical Society and, in particular, Ruth Chernia who takes my words and makes them into this book.

Althea Douglas
Ottawa, 2003

CHAPTER ONE

An Archive Is Not a Library — And What about Museums?

*"Research in archives or historical manuscript collections is unlike research in books or journal articles in libraries."**

That opening quotation is an understatement. For most of us, libraries are familiar places where finding a book is a simple and standard process — or ought to be, for books by their nature are multiples.

LIBRARIES HAVE CATALOGUES

There may be many editions, special bindings and other variations to delight bibliographers and bibliophiles, but standard cataloguing methods are meant to ensure that these will all be found together in the catalogue — be it on cards, on microfiche or in a computer. Once you have the book in hand, the table of contents, the index or the descriptive chapter headings help you to locate the facts you want.

A library's rare book room often holds manuscripts and original documents, but librarians catalogue and identify them much the same way as books. These days, students and family historians are being encouraged to use such primary material rather than relying on secondary sources (books), but finding them in a library setting is a relatively standard and familiar process. Those who want to refine their library research skills should consult *The Oxford Guide to Library Research*, a paperback edition filled with handy hints,

---

* Thomas Mann, *The Oxford Guide to Library Research* (Oxford, New York: Oxford University Press, 1998), p.260.

shortcuts and reference tools you have probably never thought of using before.

Archives Have Finding Aids

My first encounter with archives was when I was cataloguing an eighteenth century family's correspondence. Most of the letters were in the British Library or the New York Public Library. Some, however, were in the Public Record Office in London. Here I suffered severe culture shock. I was confused by mysterious and seemingly illogical arrangements of material; the familiar card catalogue was gone. Nothing worked in the way I was used to, though work it did.

It is curious how many scholars, adept at research in the largest and most complex libraries, can be totally daunted when they encounter the riches of this repository where layers of British history have been deposited by generations of officials and their clerks. An archive is not a library: "Archival institutions are receiving agencies, whereas libraries are collecting agencies. An archival institution, whether government or private, is established for the purpose of preserving materials produced by the body it serves."[1]

When you buy this book you become a "collecting agency" and, like librarians, you organize your books so they can be found when needed. If a collection of books gets big enough, it needs a sophisticated organizing system and such systems have been worked out in detail. Universities give degrees in library science, turning out graduate librarians skilled in organizing material under such systems and guiding you, the researcher, through them.

HOW ARCHIVES COME TO BE

But what are archives? Your drawer of file folders in which you keep letters and financial papers is your archive, and it will grow even with the most ruthless culling. You label folders in a way that suits you, but which others may not like. Office managers have only recently accepted the need for standard filing procedures. In past centuries the appointment of a new secretary in some ministry might see a complete change in the methods of organizing the files. Sir Hilary Jenkinson, describing how archives come to be, waxed almost lyrical:

> Archives are not collected: ... They are not there, or they should not be, because someone brought them together with the idea that they should be useful to Students of the future, or prove a point or illustrate a theory. They came together, and reached their final arrangement, by a natural process: are a growth; almost, ... as much an organism as a tree or an animal. They have consequently a structure, an articulation and a natural relationship between parts which are essential to their significance...[2]

Which is to say, archival material is not assembled to assist family historians. It is created, and following the principle of *respect des fonds*, it is maintained in its original order. How a person (or a department of government) arranges and keeps files will tell you a lot about the originator. If you want to find something in these files it helps to be familiar with the original filing systems and know how they evolved, or have lists and indexes made by someone who was knowledgeable about them.

Since each deposit is unique, each requires slightly different handling; only with the arrival of the computer did archivists have to develop standard systems for describing archives. Universities have been slow to offer degree programs in archive and record management except as an adjunct to their library schools. Until the last quarter of the twentieth century most practising archivists came into the field with experience or a degree in some related discipline, often history, and learned by doing.

How do these differences affect the researcher? Only in the degree of pre-organization of the material. Keep in mind that libraries collect books in which information has already been assembled, organized and, we hope, indexed; archives acquire files in which many separate pages containing information may or may not be fully sorted or arranged, and almost certainly are not fully indexed.

When *fonds* were measured in inches or feet of shelf space, archivists often knew the contents in detail and sometimes someone made card indexes as finding aids. The Archives of Canada's Military "C" Index is one of quite a few. Most are microfilmed and some are now entered into databases. Today, however, some government holdings fill hundreds of metres of shelf space, and no archivist can do more than itemize the series.

When I helped catalogue the Burney family correspondence (1749–1878), each and every letter and document (well over 10,000 items held in over 100 different collections, on three continents, in both libraries and archives) was inventoried separately. That effort, however, had involved a number of researchers over almost a decade, at a time when costs were a fraction of what they would be today. The end result was published as a book with a name index that fills 27 pages.[3] Most of the correspondents were English or French, and the index gives full names, dates, occupations and/or relationships, because it often included two or three generations of a family.

Some years later I found myself behind an archivist's desk, answering the questions of researchers, and came to realize what an enormous task it was to make an archival collection accessible. I had undertaken to arrange and inventory Dr. Wilder Penfield's papers for use by his biographers, which meant retaining as much as possible of Dr. Penfield's own filing systems, for these would reveal how he worked and thought. Once stored in acid-free folders and boxes, the Penfield papers filled some 85 linear feet of shelf space. To individually itemize the letters and manuscripts would, by then, have cost a small fortune. Yet this collection was minuscule compared to the holdings in our government archives or even many local repositories. It would only form a single manuscript group or, as we in Canada are supposed to say now, *fonds*. It divided into three parts: a Series of files relating to the Neurological Institute and McGill University; a larger Series of Dr. Penfield's published research papers, novels and other writing; and the third Series, files of personal correspondence.

HOW ARCHIVES ARE ARRANGED

Fonds and series, files and items are the terms the *Rules for Archival Description*[1] advise for use with true archives that have grown naturally, as described by Sir Hilary Jenkinson. The Rules are quite sniffy about "artificial accumulations of documents of any provenance brought together on the basis of some common characteristics." However, most repositories are full of these sorts of artificial accumulations. Moreover, most catalogued their collections well before the Rules were published so you will still encounter Record Groups (RG) — the material generated by an institution or government department or agency — and Manuscript Groups

(MG) — usually the personal records of an individual or association. These large basic units are then broken down into sub-groups or Series and this may be as far as a descriptive guide goes.

If time and money permit, "file lists" may be made, listing the title of each folder within a Series. Such lists (finding aids) can fill large ring binders and hunting through them for a specific item can be a slow process. In some cases file titles give a good indication of what can be found within, but they can also be totally incorrect because of some long-ago file clerk's mistake. Yet to go beyond this and inventory every item in a file is such a costly process that most archives can afford to do it for only the most important materials, such as prime ministers' papers.

Indexing of records often started in the department or agency that generated the documents. In the bad old days when a clerk copied letters into letter books, the demand "Jones! Find me that letter we wrote to Captain Fraser in Quebec two years ago!" meant that Jones (or his minions), for self-protection, made an index to the letter books. In long-established archives, such as the Public Record Office (now The National Archives) of the United Kingdom, these indexes are now part of the records and you have to call them up and consult them in order to know which letter book you want to see. Other repositories have name or subject indexes on file cards and now, more and more, such information is in the process of being transferred to a computer database that can be accessed through the Internet.

One of the joys of archival research is the wealth of peripheral information in an original deposit, but however detailed the finding aids, they can only suggest what a unique file of papers may contain. Finding aids are just that, a way of pointing out what material exists. No one expects a library catalogue card to tell what is in a book. Only a fast flip through the book's index — please let there be an index! — will tell if the author or editor has included the facts or the person you want.

No researcher should hesitate to ask for help, but you cannot expect an archivist, librarian or curator to do your research for you. They can lead you to the lists and finding aids, or check their catalogues for the material most likely to help your search. With great good luck you just might contact the archivist who has been sorting the very files you want, but don't count on it. Luck, serendipity and a memory for odd details all play a part, but only finding the right file will turn up the material you want.

ANOTHER SOURCE OF HELP

In your best local reference library ask for *Canadian State Trials Volume I: Law, Politics, and Security Measures, 1608–1837* and *Volume II: Rebellion and Invasion in the Canadas, 1837–1839*.[5] Each volume has an Appendix written by Patricia Kennedy of the Archives of Canada: Vol. I, Appendix 1, "Approaching an Iceberg: Some Guidelines for Understanding Archival Sources Relating to State Trials" and Vol. II, Appendix A, "In Pursuit of Rebels at the National Archives of Canada: Beyond the Usual Round-up of Suspect Sources."

Neither appendix is a quick or easy read, but both are filled with helpful explanations, ideas and insights distilled from years of working with eighteenth and nineteenth century records. Read and learn; the endnotes are particularly informative both about institutional infighting and warnings about the use of electronic database searching.

Never Overlook or Underestimate Museums

At the time of Canada's centennial in 1967, there was considerable impetus for both local governments and larger businesses to set up formal archives where the records of their past would be preserved. However, a century and more before that, individual antiquarians, historians, collectors and curators were doing their best to save the past and hand it on to the future. Men of influence founded local libraries or museums or historical associations, then donated collections of documents, artifacts or works of art; and persuaded friends and associates to do the same. What was collected, however, depended on individual tastes and interests, and what ends up in museum-type repositories can come as a surprise. Once you know where a family lived, a search in local and regional institutions may well turn up unexpected treasures that will enrich your family history.

In theory, archives care for the records generated by their creating institution, libraries collect books and serials, while museums look after the art and artifacts. But, in the real world, this is not necessarily so. A museum or art gallery usually has a reference library and may have established its own archive. In one or the other there may well be a large collection of manuscripts and documents. Libraries acquire photographs and artifacts, such as antique printing presses. Audio-visual material exists in most collections.

The McCord Museum of Canadian History had its origins when David Ross McCord, Q.C. (1844–1930) donated a collection of Canadian documents, art and ethnic artifacts to McGill University. Now an independent institution, the McCord's holding of documents and visual material (including the Notman Collection of Photography) is surpassed only by its ethnographic and costume collections, the latter coming as gifts from generations of wealthy and fashionable Montrealers.

In Toronto, the Royal Ontario Museum received Sigmund Samuel's extensive collection of Canadiana and the Metropolitan Toronto Library benefitted from the generosity of publisher John Ross Robertson (1841–1918).

In 1954 Eric L. Harvie established the Glenbow Foundation in Calgary where the associated Institute is a prime source of documents relating to Western Canada.[6] These gifts are but a few examples of the sorts of things that happened across Canada. Most older university libraries have been given valuable historical records and the same is true of large city libraries.

However, government policies and institutions' mandates change. In 1920, Dr. John Clarence Webster (1863–1962) retired from the Chicago Presbyterian Hospital and returned home to Shediac, New Brunswick. He devoted the rest of his life to studying and writing about the early history of the Maritime provinces, and left his rich collection of Canadiana and decorative arts to the New Brunswick Museum in Saint John. At one time, this museum cared for an extensive collection of documents relating to New Brunswick history.

When the Public Archives of New Brunswick was established in 1968, the province began to rationalize the holdings of the local institutions it supported. Some documents, such as those of local government, were transferred to Fredericton, not only from the Museum in Saint John, but from small repositories like Louise Manney's collection in Newcastle. This transfer means that citations and locations found in pre–1970 publications, may now be incorrect and, if you want to see a document, you may have to hunt around. Watch out for such record transfers in other parts of the country. For example, Ontario land records have been dispersed to whichever local repositories will care for them.

Certified copy of Registration of Birth for George Thomas Earl McCoy (author's father) born 8 January 1886, registered 10 March 1933. The birth registers for Westmorland County 1888–1919 are missing. For some reason, George McCoy needed a birth certificate in the early 1930s. "Late registration" of birth was possible in this case because George's mother was still alive and could report his birth.

CHAPTER TWO

The Whys and Wheres of Records

"An expert is someone who can cite a source that nobody else knows about."*

In this computerized era, "boiler plate" text [originally, a sheet of metal for printing from, formed by stereotyping or electrotyping a page of type] is even more common than it was in nineteenth-century weekly newspapers. My computer holds a set of formula paragraphs I use regularly when replying to family researchers:

1. Thank you for your letter of [date] requesting birth/marriage/death certificates for members of the Blank family of [Province]. I am sorry but there is very little I can do for you in Ottawa. As in the United States, the Library and Archives Canada (Ottawa) hold material relating to the country as a whole, while provinces (like your states) are responsible for records of births, marriages and deaths, as well as probate and most land transfers. Someone working in [capital city of province] and the provincial archives will be in a far better position to search for your family.

2. Except for original land grant petitions for Upper and Lower Canada, some militia lists, military service records, passenger lists after 1865, with a few earlier lists of subsidized settlers, the Library and Archives Canada in Ottawa hold very little material that relates to individual early settlers. They do have a few parish registers on film, mostly very early ones, and some from the Ottawa area, but they gave

* *Oxford Guide to Library Research* p. 43

up acquiring this sort of record several decades ago and have no systematic collection.

3. Most provincial archives hold older county and township land records, township assessment rolls, probate and other legal records, county or district marriage registers and many local church records. Other church records — which is where all births, marriages and deaths before [give date] are found — are at the archives of the various denominations, which in Ontario are mostly in Toronto (Baptists are in Hamilton).

MANY LEVELS OF GOVERNMENT

In other words, before you start researching in Canada, you need to understand that records are created and kept at different levels of government, ranging from the local municipality or township, to the county and then the province. Some are national or even international. Within the government or institutional structure they may remain at the level where they are created, at least for a time. However, the challenge is finding where they went in the next century or two.

Moreover, much as we might like it to be so, historic records were not kept for the benefit of family historians, in Canada or anywhere else. The best records were, and still are, maintained by large, hierarchical institutions, such as government departments, established churches and very large commercial enterprises. These extensive operations need such information, can afford the multitude of clerks and bureaucrats required to produce it and normally have the warehouses (which are often called Archives) to store it for a century or two after the immediate need is past.

LAND AND PROPERTY

The oldest and usually the best-kept (and indexed) sets of records concern property (primarily land), the ownership of land and the transfer of ownership by sale or inheritance. In North America, the records that survive from the early days of European settlement are, in most instances, those relating to land. This is because the Crown (i.e. the government), which in the beginning owns all land, keeps records of what is granted, who it is granted to, what the conditions of the grant are and whether or not these conditions have been met.

After the initial grant or patent is issued, however, records of the transfers of property, whether by sale, mortgage, bequest or lease, are normally held at some level of local government. If the registry office is at too great a distance, citizens cannot get to it easily and transfers may not be registered, so in most provinces the county or township keeps the books and is allowed to charge for any title searches. When there is money to be made the chance is pretty good that records will be kept, at least until they grow to a size where the cost of storage exceeds the revenue they produce. That, alas, is now well underway and century-old documents are in peril.

BIRTHS, MARRIAGES AND DEATHS

The profession of genealogy with all those quaintly named Heralds and Kings of Arms grew out of a need for western European feudal societies to keep track of who held land (at the will of the king) and so who was obliged to fight for the king. Daughters did not fight so it was the men they married who mattered. The marriage was also important because the legitimacy of any heir mattered. The established churches married, baptised and buried its parishioners and consequently were encouraged to keep records of these events from the earliest times. Some did better than others, but the Roman Catholic Church brought with it centuries of experience when it came to North America.

CHURCH RECORDS

In Quebec, vital records were kept with care, largely because in a small, isolated colony with a small population, the church had to make certain that couples who married were not too closely related. A special dispensation was required if the pair was within the prohibited degrees of consanguinity. The parish priest in New France had to be a genealogist.

The established churches of England and Scotland inherited the Roman Catholic tradition. In Britain in 1538, Thomas Cromwell issued orders that every parish clergyman should keep registers of baptisms, marriages and burials. It took over a century to get the system working and, during the Civil War and subsequent Interregnum under Cromwell [1642–60], many registers were not kept properly or were destroyed. But, after the Restoration of the king in 1660, the system of keeping parish registers worked pretty well and was exported to most British colonies. Only in eighteenth-century Nova Scotia will you find such records kept in "Town Books," a tradition nonconformist [not Church of England, Anglican] Planter settlers brought from New England. Elsewhere, the presence, or absence of clergymen will determine what was kept and where.

Settlers' cabins were often miles from any church or magistrate, but an itinerant missionary might baptise an entire family as he stopped in a settlement, returning his registers to "headquarters" in some distant city cathedral where they remained. A couple might travel a great distance, often by water, and sometimes across the border, to be married. When Native North Americans became Christians, the missionaries or parish clergy recorded their baptisms, marriages and, most importantly for their society, burial ceremonies.

Fire, flood, mould, mice and men have destroyed much, yet many early records have survived and many are now published. The originals tend to end up at a high local level, either in provincial archives or regional church archives (diocese or conference). I discuss these in chapter eight.

GOVERNMENT RECORDS

The British War Office, Admiralty, Colonial Office and Board of Trade are also hierarchical organizations that keep excellent records. Where orders and instructions descend from the top down and reports and explanations move from the bottom up, records are preserved for one basic reason that may be summed up in the words: "It's not my fault. I was only following orders!" Records of such government departments normally end up in national archives. The Archives of Canada have copied or microfilmed almost every document in Great Britain and France that relates to French and British colonial rule in what is now Canada.

More complex, but equally detailed, are judicial records. Courts may order someone to be transported or pass a death sentence, in which case detailed records are normally kept. For example, files concerning *Persons Sentenced to Death in Canada, 1867–1976: an inventory of case files in the record of the Department of Justice* are at the Archives of Canada in RG 13. The relevant Finding Aid is FA 39, typeset, spiral bound, a Government Archives Division publication that came out in 1994. It is indexed by name, year, province, victim and so on, and gives a quite detailed file content list.

HELP IS AVAILABLE

Government and judicial records usually overlap and often exist in several variants depending on who was recording what. If your errant ancestors were politically active, say around 1837 to 1839, and you find yourself in such a maze, look for *Canadian State Trials Volume II: Rebellion and Invasion in the Canadas, 1837–1839*[1] and read Patricia Kennedy's Appendix A, "In Pursuit of Rebels at the National Archives of Canada: Beyond the Usual Round-up of Suspect Sources." It offers considerable insight on how to approach and hunt for useful records. Appendix C, Susan Lewthwaite's "Rebellion Trial Sources in Ontario Archives" is also valuable.

Rebellion was rare. More common is the imposition and collecting of fines. Senior administrations do not care much about individuals but, rest assured, when money is involved, records are kept. The Courts of Quarter Session, being at the level of local government, are the exception because they were almost entirely concerned with people, their community duties and the small crimes some committed.

MONEY MAKES THE WORLD GO 'ROUND

"Don't blame me. I followed the rules!" is equally true for large business organizations and governments at every level. All are concerned with money and their outlays of funds are normally recorded in great detail, again on the principle of "It's not my responsibility; he signed for his pay here!" Hence we have muster rolls and pay lists, crew lists and agreements, tax assessment rolls and a wide variety of signed receipts and expense records.

Researchers, therefore, should expect to find surviving records tied to property, money and the transfer thereof —

did an Aboriginal ancestor act as a translator or guide? There may be a receipt for his pay. As Patricia Kennedy advises, researchers should read between the lines and use "historical imagination to develop ideas about what records might have been created, and by whom, and where they might be preserved."[2]

Where records are kept, be it head office (capital city), branch plant (county/district) or retail outlet (township office) will depend on their place of origin and how they relate to the creator, the creator's place in the hierarchy of the creating institution and the public who either used or provided information.

WHICH LEVEL OF GOVERNMENT?

Most surviving eighteenth and nineteenth century records are held by political divisions. The researcher's first challenge is to determine at which level of government they are held. This in turn demands a degree of knowledge of a government's or institution's structure during the time period when the records you need were created. This is political history, a subject most genealogists dislike, but must come to terms with. Archival finding aids almost always start with a dull and detailed explanation of who created the records and how, where and when they were created. Read it!

EXCEPTIONS THAT PROVE THE RULE

Crown grant and associated papers should be held at the national level and, yes, both Lower Canada and Upper Canada Land Papers are at the Library and Archives Canada. Why are those of Nova Scotia in Halifax? Remember that until 1867 Nova Scotia was a separate, self-governing colony and was responsible for such grants, subject to advice from the Colonial Office of course. The same holds true with the other Maritime provinces; except that New Brunswick was only separated from Nova Scotia in 1784. Grants that pre-date that split are likely to be found in Halifax. In the western provinces and territories, Crown grant papers and homestead records have been turned over to the individual provinces. A concise summary can be found in the latest edition of *Tracing Your Ancestors in Canada*, and is also available at Archives Canada's Web site.

WHAT IS THAT DOING HERE?

Occasionally items relating to local governments turn up in the "wrong" place. Perhaps they were a part of some politician's papers that he donated to his university library; possibly an official "rescued" a piece of regional history and gave it to a local museum, or even Archives Canada, because he knew someone who worked there. Don't be too surprised at what you find in the older collecting agencies; their curators were real magpies.

BUSINESS RECORDS

Where business records end up depends on these same variables and if you are hunting for such records it is even more important to know the history of the enterprise than for government records. The Hudson's Bay Company archives were considered a "national treasure" by Great Britain, and had to be completely microfilmed before they could be moved from London to Winnipeg. The Public Record Office at Kew, now The National Archives [of the United Kingdom], as well as the Library and Archives Canada hold copies of the microfilms. Permission is necessary to gain access to the records, but the finding aids are detailed and can be consulted on the Internet.

The Canadian National Railway's surviving records are at Archives Canada in Ottawa,[3] but the Canadian Pacific archives are in a sort of limbo as the focus of the company shifts. The T. Eaton Co. deposited its archival material with the Archives of Ontario. The Cunard Steamship Company archives (c.1840–1945) were deposited at Liverpool University in 1973, but early manuscripts and business papers are said to have been burnt when the firm's Halifax office and warehouse were demolished in 1911 and 1917.[4] Because biographers need such material, and hunt for it, check any biography of any founder of a firm for the sources used.

AIDS TO FINDING RECORDS

The records of smaller regional companies may well have been given to the local library, university or museum. If records were deposited before 1985 you should find them listed in the *Union List of Manuscripts in Canadian Repositories* (1975) or later *Supplements* (to 1985).[5]

These can be found in most large reference libraries. Over the following fifteen years this project stalled, waiting for better technology and computer software. The wait has ended.

CAIN BECOMES ARCHIVES CANADA

On 20 October 2001 the Canadian Council of Archives launched the Canadian Archival Information Network (CAIN) that provides access to most of the holdings of archival institutions across Canada. Then, on 17 October 2003, the Council explained that "major advancements in technology and the rapid expansion of the contents led to a relaunch of this portal under the appropriate name of Archives Canada" <www.archivescanada.ca>.

Each archival institution holding physical documents — texts, maps, artwork and more — regularly produces descriptions of these that are made available through this national database. By its nature, Archives Canada is a work in progress, but it is easy to use and should turn up the same sort of information the printed Union Lists once offered us. It will certainly be of assistance in locating records of all sorts. As more and more popular documents are digitized and added, it will make accessing records from home computers possible.

As well, many major archives make much of their inventory available on the internet, <www.usask.ca/archives> will get you to many. Even so, the modest holdings in smaller non-archival institutions can still be hard to track down.

All else failing, if the business was a local one, write to the town's public library and nearest university. Check the *Canadian Periodical Index*[6] to see if publications serving the region ran stories on businesses or prominent entrepreneurs; a regional magazine such as *The Atlantic Advocate* often holds a wealth of information on local affairs. Many newspapers also featured such stories regularly, and these have probably been clipped or indexed by the local library.

CHAPTER THREE

Microfilms and Manuscripts

*1934   Recordak Corporation introduced 35mm microfilm to
          preserve newspapers.*

*1941   "V-Mail"… a system for microfilming letters to conserve
          shipping space. Adopted for overseas communication by the
          British, by the U.S. Armed Forces in 1942.* *

MICROFILM CHANGED RESEARCH

Microfilming took off at the end of World War II and dra-
matically changed the way we research, some say for better,
some think for worse. Archivists and record managers seized
upon it as a solution to the ever-increasing mountains of
papers threatening to overwhelm them. Conservators greeted
it as the answer to the "grubby paws" syndrome slowly de-
stroying fragile documents. Scholars were able to bring together related correspondence from half a dozen collections,
and catalogue or transcribe it in their own offices, employ-
ing their own graduate students. Handling original documents is now a rare experience, but as the inter-institutional
loan system teams up with Internet indexes and catalogues,
researchers can access almost anything on microfilm or microfiche in their local library.

As enthusiasm for family history grows on both sides of
the Atlantic and avid searchers track their ancestors back in
time, more and more eager but inexperienced searchers find
themselves trying to deal with original manuscripts that have
been microfilmed or, these days, scanned and made available
electronically.

---

*   *Kodak Milestones: 1880–1980* (Rochester, NY: Eastman Kodak Co., 1980),
     pp. 13, 15.

Most archival institutions issue a sheet of instructions on the handling of original material: keep your hands clean; use only pencil; do not change the arrangement or order of the pieces of paper, parchment, or whatever; and so on.

Except for threading and focusing, very few instructions are given to the individual who is set down at a microfilm reader with a film of some passenger list, military records or hand-written manuscripts. Yet for the inexperienced searcher, microfilm, particularly films of individual sheets and fragments of documents can be very confusing, far more so than handling the actual pages. Even bound material, if oversize, can be a puzzle.

MICROFILMING: HOW IT'S DONE

When you have limited time in which to work, some under-standing of the actual microfilming process can be a big help. Normally the photographer works at a well-illuminated ta-ble where a camera is mounted in a stand, pointing down and focused on the items, placed one at a time on the flat table surface. To those who have worked with such material for years it all seems terribly obvious. Bound material is filmed one or two leaves at a time, in sequence from front to back. Loose sheets are photographed front side of the page first, then the back. If the paper is larger than the film frame, the photographer may shoot the top, the middle and the bottom, or the left side, then the right side of a document. This done, the oversize leaf is turned and the same process repeated. A long parchment strip can occupy six or more frames of film and the various shots will overlap. Check which lines are repeated and don't copy things twice.

Since the technicians doing most microfilming are rarely historians, archivists or experts on manuscripts, they will film pages in sequence from the top of the pile, as it is handed to them. If pages are out of order, or reversed so that the back of the leaf is on top, that is how it is filmed. If, for some reason, the photographer thinks there may have been too much or too little light, or a breeze fluttered the page, the shot or several shots may be repeated. Sometimes there is a note to this effect, usually not. With a little experience, you start to recognize what was going on, and look for the clearest shot.

In an ideal world, loose manuscripts would be numbered sequentially so you could tell immediately what is what. Alas, except for some runs of land papers, few manuscript collections are. Instead you rely on visual clues such as an irregular tear or folded corner, a blob of ink that shows through a page, a smear of dirt on a parchment strip. A sheet of paper that has survived a century or two tends to acquire certain unique characteristics. When you have worked with a film for some time, you will recognize pages like old friends, even when they have their backs to you.

Today, documents and manuscripts are being scanned, digitized and put onto the Internet by human beings who may not be scholars or archivists and may not recognize misplaced items. The same caveats apply as for microfilm.

READING THE UNREADABLE

Sorting out which page is which on microfilm is only the first problem. In the eighteenth century, paper was not the available commodity it is today. Official documents normally use a full sheet, but the promissory note your great grandfather gave the local storekeeper may be on a small strip torn off a larger page — and the writing may be tiny and cramped. Except for squeezed up words, however, most handwriting should not be difficult, though ink may be faded and hard to read, or the page edges may be so brown and acidic that the photographing obliterates the writing. In such cases try moving the page around in the reader, or try other readers, where the bright spot of the lamp is in a different place.

There are two tricks to dealing with mysterious words: try pronouncing the letters phonetically, several times. Inspiration may strike. With some microfilm readers you can put a sheet of paper down on the screen and trace any difficult writing, several times. Sometimes the hand recognizes letters that the eye does not.

MANUSCRIPTS

In the seventeenth and eighteenth centuries people wrote much the way we do now, but there are some differences that can cause errors. Moreover, old-fashioned writing habits seem to have persisted in North America long after they disappeared in Britain. Perhaps this was because there were fewer teachers and one or two who stuck to the old ways could influence a second and even third generation.

For example, be aware that there is a confusing form of written "e" that looks like an "o". The name really was Henry, not Honry as one family member insisted when she looked at the register entry. Many people may be familiar with the long "s" that looks like an "f" when it appears in print [ʃ]. When it turns up in handwritten text, however, it is not always recognized. In particular, it persisted when writing a double "ss" long after it was dropped from type fonts.

Caʃs, Cap, Caʃs or Cass?

In some early nineteenth century letters I once edited, a mother fed her delicate baby what we first read as apes' milk. What she had actually written was "asses' milk," using the long "ʃ" and a normal "s" that together look quite like a "p." Aʃses milk became a joke, but misreading a family name is not so funny. Once I was looking for a Cass family in a number of published indexes to parish registers. I found the name had not only been read and indexed as Carr, but since several priests used the old-fashioned long-short double ss, Caſs also turned up as Cap and once as Cals. Remember, any index is subject to human error. Check the original manuscript whenever possible.

If you trace your ancestors back to a time before the late seventeenth century, you will be confronted with texts in Latin and a script that is completely unfamiliar. In such a case you should take a course in palaeography (how to decipher early writing) and brush up your Latin.

Notice the double "s" and long "ſ" in the salutation and closing of this letter from 1861.

Transcripts, Extracts and Indexes

Original documents can be hard to read for a variety of reasons, and long lists of names in random order are difficult to search. Thus we have cause to bless those who transcribe, index and publish older records of all sorts. This has been going on extensively for over two centuries and, with the advent of personal computers in the 1980s, it took a quantum leap forward.

While researchers may bless indexers and transcribers who devote hours to making difficult to read manuscripts easy to access, when dealing with transcripts and indexes, be they of census returns, tax rolls, published directories or extracts from newspaper, always remember that they are made by human beings.

People can make mistakes — it's called human error. We all make typos, drop lines, invert numbers in a date or simply cannot read unfamiliar names if the handwriting is poor. The volunteer indexers may not know your family's names as well as you do and they may fall into archaic handwriting traps. Even professional typists, copying from microfilm and keying in text will make errors and, by the end of a fourth hour, they can average three or four typos to a page. Never proofread the fourth hour of a typist's work in the fourth hour of your proofreading session.

Garbage In, Garbage Out

How much of the material that turns up on the Internet has been proofread? Do you know how experienced the person who compiled the information is? Do you know which of several possible sources were consulted? Do you know which existing source is the more valid? Brenda Merriman's *About Genealogical Standards of Evidence* offers an excellent explanation of the many and various sorts of "facts" you might turn up, how to evaluate their credibility and how to select the sources of valid information.

THANKS — BUT TRY TO CHECK THE SOURCE

Anyone using the International Genealogical Index [IGI] is warned to check the actual register entries; this is valid advice when using any published transcript or index. If at all possible, search out the microfilms of the original record and check the actual entries. You might find mistakes in the originals; they were made by human beings. Almost always you will find additional names, perhaps in adjacent entries, that suggest relationships. Are there signatures or only Xs? Moreover, you have verified your facts one step closer to the source.

IS IT THE SAME TWICE, OR THRICE?

Be aware that records often exist in several forms. Copies of deeds or treaties are normally made for every signatory. I once had to verify the baptismal dates of several ancestors because a "cousin" had been to Yorkshire, "seen" the register and come back with different dates than I had found. This example is English, but it could apply equally in any jurisdiction where civil registration depends on lists supplied from church records. For example, you find copied registers in Quebec's Prothonotary Court records while, in other provinces, county marriage registers are based on lists the clergyman sent to the county clerk.

The parish registers of Hawnby, Yorkshire, exist in four forms: first, the original bound parish registers covering many years in each volume and microfilmed by the Record Office, so researchers would not handle the fragile originals; second, the Bishop's transcripts that were copied each year on strips of parchment and sent to the diocese offices. These were microfilmed by the LDS and can be borrowed from

Salt Lake City, but they may differ from the registers for they are a *copy*, albeit a signed and authorized copy, made each year.

A third version, a typed transcript of the Hawnby registers was made about a century ago. And fourth, the early transcripts (to 1722) were published privately and a hand-indexed copy is at the Society of Genealogists, London. The later years (after 1722) exist as typescripts in the North-allerton Record Office. These typescripts are *copies* of the original Register, and the published version is one further remove from the original.

In Yorkshire, I had seen the films of the original registers and was able to check my readings against the typescripts. Re-checking later I secured films from Salt Lake City and realized the "cousin" must have seen the films of the annually prepared Bishop's transcripts, perhaps at the Borthwick Institute where the originals are held. She had fallen into several traps set by the old calendar and the Lady Day to Lady Day "year" that persisted in preparing the Bishop's copies well after the calendar changed. She also "saw" a list of baptisms in the summer of 1755 with a clerk's D^o [ditto]:

> June 15th Joseph son of Jacob Ward
>
> D^o 23d John son of N<athan?> Williamson
>
> D^o 2<3>d Catharine daughter of Richard Pass<??>
>
> D^o 29 William son of William Chapman, Hawnby
>
> July 6th Sarah daughter of John....
>
> D^o ...

In the original manuscript, set as it is between June and July, it seems quite clear that William son of William Chapman was born on 29 June. The "cousin" claimed our mutual ancestor William was born in December and I was assured she had written down exactly what she saw. It is easy enough to see how she saw D⁰, wrote down the single entry and interpreted it as De[cember] when rereading her notes. There is a lesson to be learned here.

TIPS ON TAKING NOTES

While a printout of a page is better than any copy you can make, that is not always an option. Do not try to interpret what you are copying, especially if you are pressed for time. Always copy down *exactly* what you see; but do take the time to copy enough of any abbreviated or puzzling entry to place it in context. Try to work sequentially within a text, because the order in which entries are written down may be an essential clue when you have time to think about your findings. Scholars have a trick to avoid confusion, they use pointed brackets < > to indicate uncertain readings and square brackets [ ] to enclose their own comments on a text: for example, She told me her name was Al<ltoa>. [known to be: Althea]. Use these when making notes, you will bless yourself several years later, when, I can assure you, you will have forgotten difficulties you were certain were graven on your soul forever.

AVOID THE DREADED LOST REFERENCE

One final reminder: date your notes, write down where they were made, keep a record of the call number and the microfilm reel number. If the documents are held in an archive, note the RG or MG number and the series, volume and page numbers, so when you write that family history, you can accurately *Cite Your Sources*. This title of Richard Stephen Lackey's book has become a genealogical byword. However, for the latest advice on new media citations, see Elizabeth Shown Mills' *Evidence! Citation & Analysis for the Family Historian* (Baltimore: Genealogical Publishing Company, 1997). Following her advice will help you, and others, to find something again.

As described on its Web site, the new Gatineau Preservation Centre is a building-within-a-building. An outer shell of glass and steel creates an environmental buffer zone for the interior concrete structure which comprises preservation laboratories, records storage vaults and other operations. Photos: Denis Gagnon - Library and Archives Canada

CHAPTER FOUR

Library and Archives Canada

*"The National Library and Archives Building was opened by Prime Minister Lester B. Pearson on June 20, 1967."**

When visiting Ottawa, most family historians plan on digging for a few of their family roots at Library and Archives Canada [LAC]. This is the new name for the combined National Archives of Canada (formerly Public Archives) and the National Library of Canada. The government has finally recognized a fact known to researchers since 1967: the holdings of the National Archives and the National Library complement each other. Almost all research requires the use of both collections and, if they are in the same building, and operate in similar ways, research is easier.

True, since 1967 the two Federal institutions have been housed in the same building at 395 Wellington Street, Ottawa, Canada, but for decades they did their best to ignore each other. Sometimes it was amusing, sometimes exasperating, but with the advent of computers and electronic publishing and faced with funding cuts, cooperation between the two made better sense than defending old turf.

The first change I noticed was a rationalization of library holdings, in particular the merging of the collections of eighteenth-century serials to form more complete runs that were made available in a single reading room. This was a small, intelligent move that was a big help to users. From

---

* *National Library of Canada* (Ottawa: Minister of Supply and Services Canada, 1982), p.10.

preliminary plans now posted on the Internet, more of the same are on the way.

Once the enabling legislation is passed by Parliament, the amalgamated Library and Archives will be responsible for Canada's documentary heritage. (As we go to press, the legislation has not passed.) Documentary heritage is a new concept that may change the way we approach research. As explained on their Web site:

> The wording of the legislation has been updated to be forward-looking and technology neutral. This will ensure that the traditional published and unpublished forms of Canadian documentary heritage, regardless of the media used to create them, will be preserved and made available to Canadians now and in the future.

Regardless of the medium used!

Parchment rolls, illuminated manuscripts, printed books, hand-written documents, painted portraits, typed copies, photographs, recorded sound, microfilm, mixed media, computer databases, electronic publishing on CDs, digitized documents and whatever may come next will all be found in the collection of this single institution.

Amalgamation makes sense. Information is information however it is presented, so the old divisions — libraries collect multiples, archives receive unique deposits — breaks down when facing the growing variety of ways in which we can document our heritage. Nevertheless, the old ways will not change overnight. Rules of description and cataloguing are set and accepted, call numbers are on millions of books, finding aids are printed, miles of archival storage boxes are already labeled with MG and RG numbers. But the number of computer-searchable catalogues and databases available on the Internet is growing every day. Researchers can do much of their preliminary work at home on their own computers.

Change comes slowly. Employees of the new institution will continue to "facilitate the management of information in government institutions" and be the "permanent repository of Government of Canada records," doubtless wearing archivists' hats. The institution will continue the "existing National Library roles and responsibilities" wearing librarians' hats. So, for convenience during the years of transition, this book will refer to the Archives of Canada and the Library of Canada, remembering that they are already thinking along the same lines when it comes to newer media. The quotations are taken from "Backgrounder" on the Archives of Canada's Web site, as of 1 June 2003. Check the Web sites regularly for the latest information on the progress and details of amalgamation.

The Library Reading Room and Reference desk are still on the second floor, the Archives Reference section and Reading room are on the third floor, but both now have the same opening hours. A single bar-coded user card valid for both Library and Archives can be obtained at the ground-floor registration desk. There is one difference, the Archives' Postal Code is still K1A 0N3, the Library's is K1A 0N4.

One similarity is that as each collection expands, more material is held off site and may take a day or two to retrieve. If your time is limited, write or call and ask about pre-ordering material. Even if you never get to Ottawa, this national institution offers services to all Canadians and to family historians on both sides of the border, as well as overseas. The Library and Archives both participate in the International Inter-library (or Inter-institution) Loan program that will bring material to your local library from almost anywhere.

LIBRARY OF CANADA — LEGAL DEPOSIT

Canadian publishers are required to deposit at the Library two copies (or one if only 3 to 101 copies are made) of all books, pamphlets, serial publications (added 1965), microforms (added 1988), spoken word sound recordings (added 1969), video recordings, electronic publications issued in physical formats (CD-ROM, CD-I, computer diskette etc.; added 1993), and one copy of musical sound recordings (added 1969) and multimedia kits (added 1978). The latest modernization of the mandate will include collecting online publications and a "sampling from the Internet." It adds up to many "publications" every year, and although not every small, privately printed book makes its way to the Library, a surprising number do.

The Library publishes *Canadiana* (the national bibliography) that lists publications produced in Canada or relating to Canada. This was originally issued in microfiche format, then on CD-ROM, with the information also available on the Internet through AMICUS. AMICUS is the union catalogue, which is searchable online and lists most holdings of major Canadian libraries. Thus it includes data from earlier research tools issued on fiche (and CD-ROM), the *Union List of Canadian Newspapers* and the *Union List of Serials in the Social Sciences and Humanities*. If the Library does not have a particular book or serial, it will advise you where it can be found.

The Library's pre-Confederation (before 1867) collection is extensive, having over time absorbed the older holdings of the Library of Parliament, rationalized collections with the National Archives Library and acquired many special collections either by donation or purchase. Through AMICUS you can locate other rare volumes in various Canadian institutions.

CIHM - ICMH

As well, we have the Canadian Institute for Historical Microreproductions (Institut Canadien de microrepro-ductions historiques, CIHM-ICMH). This independent, non-profit institute was founded in 1978 to identify, locate and microfilm a Canadiana collection that was to be as com-prehensive as possible, making rare and scarce material more widely available.

Today the numbers are awesome: Pre-1900 Monographs, 57,840 titles on 122,800 microfiche; Canadian Directories, 464 titles on 4,136 microfiche — this is a sub-set of the Pre-1900 Annuals Collection of 2,431 titles. Then there is the Pre-1900 Periodicals Collection, still in the process of being brought together from assorted library stacks, museum attics and historical society basements, estimated to be about 55,000 issues. Because they are on fiche, your local librarian can probably secure a copy of almost any title for you, however rare and fragile the original, and printouts can also be made.

Ask about securing a catalogue or "Short Title Listing" for your subject segment of the Collection. A bibliography covering CIHM titles relating to *Genealogy and Local History to 1900*[1] compiled by Brian Gilchrist and Clifford Collier is available from the OGS.

ARCHIVES OF CANADA

The National Archives of Canada Act, proclaimed in 1987, changed the name of the Public Archives of Canada [PAC] to the National Archives of Canada [NA] and updated the Public Archives Act of 1912. That earlier legislation had made official a service that had been developing as the Archives Branch of the Department of Agriculture since 1872.[2] In the fifty years before that, individual initiatives to save and collect Canada's documented history were assisted by the various colonial governments, so some material still rests in provincial archives.

Like any national collection, the Archives of Canada's holdings range over a vast assortment of media, formats and centuries and, during the 1980s particularly, the PAC/NA published a lot of booklets and brochures describing their collections and activities. Among the most extensive was a "General Guide Series," which came out in the early 1980s. These older booklets outline the holdings of their Manuscript Division, the one of most interest to genealogists, as well as the Government Archives Division, the Documentary Art and Photography Division, the Map Division and the Sound and Moving Images Division.

The names of these groupings has recently been changed. The Government Archives Division has become the Government Records Branch (GRB), the Manuscript Division has become the Canadian Archives Branch (CAB), and within CAB there are a Cartographic and Architectural Division (formerly the National Map Collection) and an Audio-Visual Division (National Film and Sound Division). The Documentary Art and Photography Division has become the Art and Photography Division while portraits, in whatever medium, will go to the National Portrait Gallery.

Another series of guides describes records relating to various nationalities who came as settlers and, yet another, the holdings of some individual Government Departments. In 1990 neat little brochures explained what *The London Office* and *The Paris Office* were doing, followed by *The National Archives Act* (1992), *Using Archives* (1993) and *The Canadian Postal Archives* (1993).

Currently these earlier booklets can be found on the Archives' Web site under "Publications," or you can write and ask about any that interest you. When you write, ask for the Archives' free booklet *Tracing your Ancestors in Canada*, which was updated in 2001. Although you can find the same material on the Internet <www.archives.ca>, the booklet is a small and very helpful reference to have at hand. It includes bibliographies, useful addresses, provincial probate and vital statistics information, a list of existing census records and the latest information on the releases of immigration and naturalization records.

LONDON AND PARIS

Soon after the Public Archives of Canada was established in 1872, offices were opened in both London and Paris to locate and copy documents relating to Canada in both mother countries. Between 1883 and 1945 successive teams of researchers in Paris copied by hand 450,000 pages of French records, while in London similar work would produce over 650 linear feet of transcripts. With the introduction of microfilming in the 1950s the volume of copying increased greatly. The following decades saw teams spreading out from the capitals to delve for North American material in regional repositories.

Speaking as a researcher, the hand-copied documents may have errors in transcription, but the handwriting is usually easier to read than many originals. Either will give details of the world your ancestor lived in. Historian Christopher Moore, in his *Louisbourg Portraits: Life in an Eighteenth-Century Garrison Town*, was able to use French records to give us "Five dramatic, true tales" of actual people who lived in the French fortress-town on Cape Breton then called Île Royale. He explains that eighteenth-century France had a very centralized government. To keep the central authorities informed Colonial officials regularly compiled dossiers on every aspect of their duties and written reports, shipping manifests, maps, plans, censuses and statistics were copied in duplicate or triplicate, and sent back to France on different ships. The habits of the government hierarchy spread to the notaries and priests who diligently kept copies of documents and witnessed and compiled registers of baptisms, marriages and burials. The law courts preserved verbatim transcripts of even trivial cases. "Record-keeping was in the nature of the society."[3]

As genealogists we can only be thankful, for this applies to all of France's American possessions. If the copy in the colony was lost, there may well be another in France, and so perhaps a copy or microfilm among the NAC Manuscript Division's holdings. Here MG 1 through MG 9 are records of the French regime, including archives of the ministries of colonies, marine, war and foreign affairs. Quite a lot of the finding aids to these French records are now available on-line.

British administrators may not have been quite as assiduous record keepers, but they nevertheless generated a lot of paper. The Manuscript Division's MG 11 is the Colonial Office, and here you find scattered lists of subsidized settlers; MG 12 is Admiralty and MG 13 the War Office. The Audit Office (MG 14) and Treasury (MG 15) records are where you find the raw data on Loyalist claims, but much of this has been abstracted and published. As of mid-2003, very little British colonial material is on-line, but it will come.

Among the records of the colonies that became Canada, among the best preserved are the papers relating to land grants. The Indexes to the Upper Canada and the Lower Canada Land Papers (1764–1841) as well as the papers themselves can be obtained on microfilm. The early Land Petition files sometimes hold fascinating information; see page 45, "Start with Land."

Canadian Genealogy Centre Web Site

This Web site was launched on Saturday, 29 March 2003: <www.genealogy.gc.ca>, or use the links from the archives <www.archives.ca> or library <www.nlc-bnc.ca> pages. Initially it is designed to provide links to a multitude of Canadian Web sites relating to genealogy. In cooperation with Library and Archives Canada, digitized documents and other research material will also be made available and, using these, indexing projects are already underway. There has been ongoing consultation with potential users and genealogical organizations and, as it grows and develops, the site will almost certainly be a valuable tool for both the amateur family historian and the professional researcher.

The Canadian Genealogy Centre is virtual at the moment, and the site is being built up slowly and with care. For the foreseeable future the Library and the Archives Web sites will remain the place where you do much of your on-line research, but this will change. As the Library and the Archives merge into one research institution, so will their Internet presence. Do explore all three sites, keep ongoing notes on what you find useful and expect services to expand.

International Inter-institutional Loan System

While more and more rare books and documents are being digitized and posted on the Internet, I never cease to be amazed at what can be obtained through the international inter-institutional loan system. The essential facts your librarian or archivist needs to secure material you may want from the Library and Archives Canada are posted on the Internet. For the library: <www.nlc-bnc.ca> then go to "Services," then "Services for Libraries"; for the archives <www.archives.ca> and click on "Services," then either "Borrowing microfilm" or "Copies of Records."

An Index of Land Claim Certificates of
Upper Canada Militiamen Who Served in the War of 1812-1814

continued   **File 30: pp.248-395**

PAGES	NAME	UNIT
260-265	John Fairman	1st Regiment Prince Edward Militia
266-270	Wallis S. Fairman	Provincial Marine
271-274	William Fairman	Flank Company 1st Regiment Hastings Militia
275-276	Francis Falkner	1st Flank Company 1st Regiment Glengarry Militia
277-278	Ralph Falkner	1st Flank Company 1st Regiment Glengarry Militia
279-284	Ralph Falkner	Provincial Light Cavalry
285-286	Samuel Falkner	1st Flank Company 1st Regiment Glengarry Militia
287-290	Samuel Falkner	Provincial Light Cavalry
291-294	William Falkner	Provincial Light Dragoons
295-298	Samuel Fagerson	1st Flank Company 2nd Regiment Leeds Militia
299-300	Archilus Farnum	1st Flank Company 2nd Regiment Leeds Militia
301-302	John Farnum	1st Flank Company 2nd Regiment Leeds Militia
303-304	Pierre Feanon	Kingston Dock Yard
305-306	Jacob Feader	1st Flank Company 1st Regiment Dundas Militia
307-310	Frederick Felker	1st Regiment 4th Regiment Lincoln Militia
311-312	David Fell	Flank Company 1st Regiment Grenville Militia
313-314	Frederick Fell	Flank Company 1st Regiment Grenville Militia
315-316	John Fell	Flank Company 1st Regiment Grenville Militia
317-318	Daniel Fennel	Kent Volunteers
319-322	Jacob Fenner	Incorporated Militia
323-324	Archibald Ferguson	2nd Flank Company 5th Regiment Lincoln Militia
325-327	Donald Ferguson	1st Flank Company 1st Regiment Glengarry Militia
328	Farington Ferguson	1st Regiment Prince Edward Militia
329-332	Hugh Ferguson	Provincial Light Dragoons
333-337	Israel Ferguson	1st Regiment Prince Edward Militia
338-339	John Ferguson	1st Flank Company 1st Regiment Glengarry Militia
340-341	John Ferguson Jr	1st Flank Company 1st Regiment Glengarry Militia
342-343	John Ferguson	Flank Company 1st Regiment Stormont Militia
344-347	Joseph Ferguson	Incorporated Militia
348-351	Philemon Ferguson	1st Flank Company Prince Edward Militia
352-353	Richard Ferguson	Flank Company 2nd Regiment York Militia
354-355	Daniel Ferrer	1st Flank Company 2nd Regiment Leeds Militia
356-359	Casey Ferris	Flank Company 1st Regiment Frontenac Militia
360-361	Daniel Ferris	Flank Company 1st Regiment Frontenac Militia
362	Isaac Ferris	(See Vol.18: pages 366-367 on p.3)
363	John Ferris	(See Vol.18: pages 366-367 on p.3)
364-365	Willet Ferris	Flank Company 1st Regiment Frontenac Militia
366-367	John Fetterly	Flank Company 1st Regiment Stormont Militia
368-369	Peter Fetterly	1st Regiment Dundas Militia
370-373	Rudolph Fetterly	1st Flank Company 1st Regiment Stormont Militia
374-376	Benjamin Feve	Incorporated Militia
377-378	Edward Fidler	Kingston Dock Yard
379-383	Alexander Field	Incorporated Militia
384-385	David Fields	Niagara Light Dragoons
386-387	David Fields	Kent Volunteers
388-389	George Fields	Kent Volunteers
390-391	George Fields	Provincial Light Dragoons

continued

32

from an index compiled by Wilfred R. Lauber for the Ontario Genealogical Society,© 1995

CHAPTER FIVE

Where Oh Where? Try an Index

INDEX	1. an alphabetical list of names, subjects, etc., with references, usu. at the end of a book…
DIRECTORY	1. a book, listing alphabetically or thematically 2. a particular group of individuals (e.g. telephone subscribers)…

The *Oxford Encyclopedic English Dictionary* gives nine meanings for the noun "index," but it is the first definition that strikes a chord with genealogical researchers: an alphabetical list of names. An alphabetical list of names can be scanned very quickly to see if the people you care about are in it. And since this is Canada, you should be able to recognize these lists in either official language:

répertoire	[rɛpertwaːr] **m** alphabetical list, index, directory
fichier	**m** card file index, data file
annuaire	**m** directory published annually (e.g. telephone book)

WHERE DO YOURS COME FROM?

To find a family in census or other name lists or to find newspaper obituaries and cemetery inscriptions, you need to know where your ancestor lived; not just the province, but at least the county and even the township or, if they lived in a large city, the street address and the ward or electoral district it is in.

Alphabetical lists of people are where you look first: city and county directories, telephone books, lists of school or college graduates, directories of professions or trades or, in the early days of settlement when these did not exist, your fall backs are indexes of land grants and records of marriages.

INDEXES OF INDEXES — THE PEOPLE OF …

If you have no idea where an ancestor lived in what is now Canada, and if that ancestor has at least one distinctive name — perhaps Xenophon Cougle, Elihu MacDonald or Longley Willard — you should consult a series published by the Genealogical Research Library in Toronto, and now available as a searchable database on CD, titled *Canadian Genealogy Index, 1600s–1900s: From the Genealogical Research Library* (Novato CA: Broderbund software, c.1996).

The first three-volume set was entitled *People of Ontario 1600–1900* and a second three-volume set covered *The French Canadians 1600–1900*. This should have been entitled "The People of Quebec" because it includes both language groups. There followed three-volume sets covering *The Central Canadians*, which included residents of both Ontario and Manitoba, so cross-check with the earlier Ontario set; *The Atlantic Canadians*; and *The Western Canadians* covering Alberta, British Columbia, Saskatchewan, the Northwest Territories, Yukon and Alaska, since one source was a 1901 directory listing people in both the Yukon and Alaska during the gold rush.[1]

Each set is a cumulative index to a variety of sources relating to the region or parts of the region. Each claims to cover three centuries from 1600 to 1900, though most sources are nineteenth century. They include older county and business directories, subscription lists from county histories or atlases, and a few early census and tax rolls. The entries will point you to these sources and you can work outward from them.

The commoner the names, the less helpful these indexes are, though if family tradition indicates the province and a city or township, check what sources the above books have indexed and look for newer publications of a similar sort. These are coming out regularly and the main problem today is finding what's new out there waiting to simplify your research.

One warning about family tradition: do not confuse townships with towns or cities that have the same name. I have discussed the various same-name and changed-name traps in detail in *Here be Dragons*.

If using a computerized library catalogue, start under "subject" with the name of the place, preferably at the township level, and check out anything classified as "genealogy," "biography" and even "history." If you can find nothing at this level, check the county. Then try typing in the standard subject heading: "Registers of births etc. — Province — Place Name." As well, try to find Internet pages dealing with research in your specific area. Often they can point you to privately held indexes available directly from the compiler.

Chapter one suggested consulting *The Oxford Guide to Library Research*; have a look at the Guide's chapter nine, "Published Bibliographies." As more and more historical material is transcribed, indexed and published, knowing how to use such tools will speed up research.

DIRECTORIES

Directories come in many forms; your local library will have a selection of telephone books, as well as books listing school or university graduates, professions and trades, actors, archivists, educators, writers, musicians, engineers and even genealogists.

Directories in Print, published annually by Gale Research Inc.,[2] lists more than 15,000 directories published in the United States, United Kingdom, Canada and Australia.[3]

WARNING: Many of the directories that you find in libraries may be out of date, particularly the addresses and job positions. Older lists may be exactly what you want, but make sure to note the edition and date of publication.

INDEXES OF RESIDENTS

City directories provide name, address and often occupation. Farmers' directories give name, lot location and post office. Urban centres are better served than rural areas but these are not a bad place to start looking for grandfather or great-grandfather — grandmother is another matter entirely.

Early directories, both city and county, were prepared for and sold to businessmen, and tended to include those people businessmen might want to reach: other businessmen, tradesmen, farmers, but not often labourers. After 1867 the compilers often tried to include all male inhabitants over the age of 18. Women who were proprietors of businesses are usually included; widows turn up quite regularly and by 1900 women working outside the home may be listed. Wives names start to be shown only in the 1930s or 1940s. Jane MacNamara offers helpful information and tips on research in directories in "Using commercial directories for family history research," *Toronto Tree*, vol. 29, no. 2 (March/April 1998).

The first city directory in Canada was published in 1790: *Directory of the City and Suburbs of Quebec*. A second edition came out in 1791, but nothing further appeared until 1822. Montreal's first directory dates from 1819; York's (Toronto) from 1833, but publication was sporadic and the runs appear incomplete. By Confederation, however, you will find annual directories for the large cities as well as rural or county farmers' directories. The National Library's bibliography *Canadian Directories, 1790–1987*[1] tells what exists and where it is held. The listings in the *Genealogy and Local History to 1900/ … Bibliography*, from the CIHM-ICMH, indicates which are available in microform and so can be obtained through inter-institutional loan services. Western Canadian Directories on microfiche and microfilm is a useful finding aid for that part of Canada.[5] Be aware that gazetteers and atlases may include directories, eg. Smith's 1867 *Eastern Townships Gazetteer and General Business Directory*,[6] which described every community, large and small, also lists businesses and many residents.

WARNING: Even today some people refuse to give information to canvassers — and canvassers are human and can mishear or misspell names. Alas, you cannot verify directory sources, but you can check entries over several years, often over many years. Once telephone service comes, you can cross-check names and addresses in the telephone directories, many back issues of which are available on microfiche. Most local libraries have a set for their city or region.

BEFORE DIRECTORIES

Long before directories, however, records were being kept of land ownership and marriage, because these mattered to both church and state. If your ancestors were early settlers in British colonies, look first to the land. In French settlements, look to the church.

START WITH LAND

Except for seigneurial land in Quebec, knowing the township, range or concession and lot number is important for family research in any part of British North America. If your family arrived before the 1850s, the best index to start with is the Archives of Canada's index to Upper and Lower Canada land papers. This includes petitions, grants and related documents and was indexed years ago. Both the card index and the actual papers are available on microfilm from the LAC and in other repositories. It is a slow process to find the right index film (specify surname[s] and province), then the reels with the actual documents. Copying on a reader-printer is authorized.

Lower Canada/Canada East (Quebec): In the surveyed townships, land tends to be granted to groups of "Associates," however, lists of the individual Quebec land grants were published in the *Journal of the Legislative Assembly* (Lower Canada) 1949, Volume 8, Appendix 3, divided by county and township, then by range and lots, and giving the name. In addition, there are nominal listings of grantees by township — quick if you know the township, a long hunt if you do not.

Upper Canada/Canada West (Ontario): Papers relating to the initial Crown grant are usually those of the individual petitioner and often quite informative, but they do not always indicate the actual piece of land granted. However, the Archives of Ontario has prepared a computer generated index of each initial Crown grant, lease or sale by a land company and the printouts, by township (concession and lot number) and by name of individual are widely available on microfiche. The name section of this *Ontario Land Record Index* (OLRI) may well locate members of your family and where they held land in Ontario.

WARNING: The tables are computer generated, so following Concession 1, you will find 10, 11, 12, etc., then nos. 2–9. For a detailed explanation see Merriman, *Genealogy in Ontario*, pages 93–99.

In the Atlantic provinces, original land grants and indexes are at the individual provincial archives. Those for New Brunswick are on-line through the Provincial Archives of New Brunswick Web site. Consult the *Genealogist's Handbook for Atlantic Canada Research* [hereafter Handbook for Atlantic Canada][6] and start planning a summer research holiday or contact a local researcher who can delve for you.

The prairie provinces have a different form of land survey, so you must become familiar with new meanings for ranges and townships as well as sections and quarter-sections when you approach the "address" problem. Homestead registers, files and indexes were deposited with the respective provincial archives or land registrar.[8]

INDEXES IN NEW FRANCE AND ACADIA

The French who settled here before the British conquest include those who settled in Acadia (which became Nova Scotia, New Brunswick and Prince Edward Island) and those who came to Canada or New France (now Quebec and Ontario). The published Acadian records are detailed in the *Handbook for Atlantic Canada*, and include guides to families, family names and family histories.

RÉPERTOIRE DES …

For Roman Catholic families in Quebec, regardless of language (French, English or Gaelic), the many *Répertoires des mariages…* are easy to use. There are two marriage indexes, Drouin and Loiselle, that cover the whole provinc e and bordering areas. The *Fichier Loiselle*, a card index of marriages, 1642–1963, prepared by Père Antoine Loiselle, is in microform as a set of microfiche that fill four file drawers, two for the women's names, two for the men. Take care, however, the names are alphabetical by surname but then, *alphabetical by surname of spouse* rather than first name.

The Institut Généalogique Drouin also indexed marriages[9]: each of the over one hundred volumes has two sections, related (but not always) to the marriage date, alphabetical by surname, then by first (Christian) name, then by surname of spouse. Be sure to check both sections of each volume.

In addition, there are published marriage indexes for specific counties and countless parishes; these normally give marriage date, parish and the names of the parents of the bride and groom. Some entries even give the parents' parishes if different from where the marriage took place. Start with a known couple, find their marriage and, with luck, you can trace a family line back to seventeenth-century France very quickly. It is a great temptation to do so and boast of the results. However, I have found enough errors and missing entries, that I could never advise accepting these secondary sources as proof positive.

BEFORE 1799 YOUR WORK IS DONE

For dates prior to 1799 the *Programme de recherche en démographie historique (PRDH)*[10] has indexed every Roman Catholic baptism, marriage and burial, as well as the surviving census returns, and made the data available on compact disks and on the Internet. It is probably as accurate as any extracted database can be, but it never hurts to check the original. All Quebec church registers to 1899 are available on microfilm. While the published volumes (1621–1765) are somewhat tricky to use, *R.A.B. du PRDH: repertory of the baptism, marriage and burial certificates of 17th-18th century*, Quebec is now available on CD-ROM (P.R.D.H. Release 1.10b, Boucherville QC: G. Morin).

Particularly useful for twentieth-century Quebec are two CD-ROM databases: *Index consolidé des décès du Québec, 1926–1996* and *Index consolidé des mariages du Québec, 1926–1996* — version 1.2 (Sainte-Foy, QC: Société de généalogie de Québec, c. 2000). These include all citizens, both Roman Catholic and "Others," and have been available on microfilm for many years, but are far easier to use as a database. Just remember that women tend to retain their maiden names in the official record of death.

P.E.I. MASTER NAME INDEX

The Public Archives and Records office [PARO] of Prince Edward Island holds a Master Name Index,[11] in two series, compiled from all island gravestones, nearly all extant censuses, marriage bonds and licenses, inquest records, petitions, various church and school records and a wide range of published directories, newspapers, local and family histories, etc. The index cards, arranged alphabetically by family name, then by personal name, fill 60 reels of 16mm film that are available at the PARO. Library and Archives Canada has a full set, as does the Toronto Reference Library. The latter once issued a three-page guide. However, the films do not appear to be available elsewhere outside of PEI.

NEW BOOKS OF NAMES

Two quite recently published works may not turn up in older handbooks. E. R. Seary, *Family Names of the Island of New-foundland* is now out in a new corrected edition.[12] A new tool for Acadian research is the first part of a *Dictionnaire généalogique des familles acadiennes* that covers the years 1636–1714 in 2 volumes.[13]

INTERNET ANYONE?

Internet access to index databases is growing apace, but it comes with a caution: be sure you are certain what is indexed and what is not included. The OGS's *Index to the 1871 Census of Ontario*, a database for the entire province can be searched for heads of households and strays, but not every family member. You will find it at the Archives of Canada Web site <www.archives.ca> where you can also determine if a man served with the Canadian Expeditionary Force during World War I — well, most of the time.

While it is growing every day, "Not yet complete" describes many of the database indexes of the Archives' holdings. It will be years before you can forget about using the published guide series and the red and blue ring-binders at the LAC that direct you to further finding aids.

AMICUS, the library's union catalogue, covering their holdings and the collections in other Canadian libraries is probably as complete as possible under the circumstances. But not every publisher complies with Legal Deposit rules. The same can be said of the Canadian Expeditionary Force of World War I. The archivists who deal with it have admitted to me that a small number of soldiers' files somehow have managed to drop through the cracks and cannot be found. If the soldier died, the Commonwealth War Graves Commission also has a Web site with a searchable index: <www.cwgc.ca>.

The Archives has an excellent database of post offices and postmasters for all of Canada. This is great for finding obscure or ghost towns in rural areas, as well as each and every postmaster, their dates of service and, often, other information. One assumes this is a complete database, but there are others on the Archives' Web site that are still being worked on.

Recently, volunteers from the British Isles Family History Society of Greater Ottawa have been building a database on Home Children using the Archives holdings of passenger lists. As of mid-2002 only "about half the records" had been transcribed and entered into the database, although this much can be searched on the Archives' Web site.[14] John Sayres and his team are doing fine work, but it is not finished yet. An informative article by historian Dave De Brou, "Home Truth" in *The Beaver*, tells of solving the mystery of his grandfather's origins while showing his students how to use the Archives' searchable databases.[15]

Ontario and British Columbia cemetery indexes are searchable on the Internet (see chapter ten). British Columbia's nominal indexes to provincial vital records — marriages into the 1920s and deaths through the 1970s — can be checked at <www.bcarchives.gov.bc.ca>. Manitoba Vital Statistics (births over 100 years ago, marriages more than 80 years ago and deaths, 70 years ago) can be searched on the government site <web2.gov.mb.ca/cca/vital/Query.php>. The Canadian Genealogy Centre <www.genealogy.gc.ca> has posted data from Grosse Île records, and you should check that site regularly for further goodies.

The Archives of New Brunswick has a Web site with a number of searchable indexes: to land records, to biographical entries in several books and directories and to certain Irish immigrants. Be sure to read the introductions and be certain you know what exactly was being indexed and what was not indexed.

At <automatedgenealogy.com/census/intro.html> you will find a project in progress to index the 1901 census of New Brunswick. You should check with care just what census districts are included. Some of the site is open, other portions are commercial, so be warned.

Yet another warning about what is not indexed: there is a database available both on the Internet and on CD-Rom, *Ships and Seafarers of Atlantic Canada: The Atlantic Shipping Project* (St. John's, Nfld: Maritime History Archive, Memorial University of Newfoundland, c.1998). Begun in the early 1970s, it indexed only ten ports in Atlantic Canada. It misses as many more that became ports of registry after Confederation. It may include your shipbuilding and seafaring ancestors or it may not. Here is one example: Robert Andrew Chapman built ships at Rockland, New Brunswick, in the 1870s. As long as Saint John was the closest port of registry for him, his ships are in the database. When Dorchester, just across the river from Rockland became a port of registry, Chapman ships drop out of the database, even though the shipyard remained busy.

You probably will not find your sailor ancestors either, which is not to say they did not exist. The names of seafarers are a limited "selection" taken from records of only the ten ports indexed.

CHAPTER SIX

Lists of Names

"And it came to pass in those days, that there went out a decree from Caesar Augustus, that all the world should be taxed." (Luke 2:1)

OFFICIAL LISTS

If we think of all the lists of names bureaucrats have created over the centuries, among the most useful to family historians are tax rolls, militia lists and census returns. The good news is that such documents are official contemporary records of people living at a given time in a given place. The bad news is that most are based on geographic divisions, few are alphabetical, the original handwriting can be difficult to read, ink may be faded, the paper damaged and portions missing. Searching the original documents for your James Smith can be a long and tedious task; finding it transcribed, indexed and published is a dream that is coming true more and more, but not always. Census and militia records are better served than tax rolls.

CENSUSES

As official lists of names go, census returns are probably the ultimate genealogical tool, however, censuses come in a variety of forms and it may be helpful to define the terminology.

AGGREGATE ENUMERATIONS

A simple head-count of population, or portion of the population, is often called a "census" and is almost useless to family historians. The records of our aboriginal people include many such head counts.

HEAD-OF-HOUSEHOLD RETURNS

Most censuses taken in the late eighteenth and early nineteenth century name only the head of the household; other occupants were counted along with the livestock. Age and gender groups may indicate how many males of military age, women of child-bearing age or children requiring schooling were in the population.

AGRICULTURAL RETURNS

These can be either a type of census or a tax roll. The owner of land is named in connection with his farm, perhaps how much it produces or its valuation. These usually give the lot number, concession number or other land designations that constitute the address. Except for the occasional widow heading a family or a rare land-owning spinster, women are seldom named in either tax rolls or early census records. On the other hand, the details of individual farm production can shed fascinating light on your ancestors' lives.

NOMINAL CENSUS RETURNS

These name every individual and record such details as age, sex, marital status, place of birth, religion, etc., and begin around 1851 in most British North American colonies. Their format and questions vary with the colony until 1871 when the newly formed Dominion of Canada instituted a uniform nominal census that has been taken every decade since. The questions asked vary with the political concerns of the decade in which they are asked. Check whether the agricultural schedules have survived for your parts of the country.

Early Censuses

Early French colonial censuses are nominal. They were first taken in Quebec 1666 and 1667 on the orders of Louis XIV of France. These and the 1681 census were part of the PRDH database and are incorporated in René Jetté's *Dictionnaire généalogique des familles du Québec*.[1]

The earliest census for Acadia dates from 1671. In Newfoundland, there were several early French lists as well as English lists of inhabitants made in 1675, 1676 and 1677. Extant census records for Atlantic Canada are listed in the provincial sections of the *Handbook for Atlantic Canada*, but note that Acadian records are found in the "Acadians" section.

Nova Scotia's 1851 and 1861 censuses are by head of household, but those for New Brunswick are nominal. Prince Edward Island's early returns survive only in fragments, but these, as well as the Island's 1891 census, are included in the Master Name Index.

Quebec took head-of-household censuses in 1825, 1831 and 1842 (this last has a space for the length of time the settler had been in the province); Ontario in 1842 and 1848. All have been microfilmed. But, regarding Ontario, a book whose title promises more than it provides is *1848 and 1850 Canada West (Ontario) Census Index: An Every-Name Index*.[2] It is actually an index to surviving fragments of returns from Huron, Johnstown and Newcastle Districts of Ontario, not held at the Archives of Ontario and not readily available on microfilm.

Census Information in Print

For the nineteenth and early twentieth century, *Tracing Your Ancestors in Canada* includes a tabulation of census records by province. A fuller one is in the Appendix to the LAC's *Catalogue of Census Returns on Microfilm 1666-1891*.[3] The 1901 census takes another book, *Catalogue of Census Returns on Microfilm, 1901*.[4] The main texts list the villages, towns, townships and counties within each province, and gives the number of the microfilm reel(s) on which the returns for each census year appear.

CENSUS INFORMATION ONLINE

The two published catalogues of census returns on microfilm have been combined into a searchable database for all census films, 1666–1901. This is available in the "Genealogy: Census" section at the Archives Web site <www.archives.ca> where you will find everything you want or need to know in the "Online Help." It includes a list of provincial institutions that hold census microfilms, what years are available for each province and the "Dates of Census Enumerations." This last is particularly useful when calculating approximate birth dates from census ages, or when tracking ancestors who moved a lot.

One very helpful hint the Archives' page gives is to use their searchable "Post Offices and Postmasters" database to look up small communities. The entry will give the federal electoral district that usually corresponds to the county and census district.

Returns and Indexes Online

The 1901 census has been scanned, digitized and is posted on the Archives Web site, however, it is not indexed by name, only by place. The latest records to be released are those of 1906. The "Census of the Northwest Provinces, 1906," covers Manitoba, Saskatchewan and Alberta and is also digitized and on the Archives' Web site.

The Index to the 1871 Census of Ontario can be searched on the Archives Web site. The 1881 Census of Canada has been issued by the LDS Family History Library, and is available on their Web site as well as on a CD that you can buy or find at the Library and Archives of Canada. Several provincial genealogical societies have indexed local census returns; some are online. Check the societies' Web sites for details.

TAX ROLLS

Census records are limited for the early settlements of British North America, but governments often kept tax rolls. In particular, there are a number of poll tax and assessment rolls covering much of Nova Scotia, most of which date from 1791–1795. These list men over age 21 and the capitation tax they should pay. Needless to say, some men tried to avoid being listed and paying; sixpence was a large sum of money in those days. Dates and microfilm numbers are found in the LAC's *Census Returns on Microfilm* (most are on M-5219). Terrence M. Punch lists other Nova Scotia lists of names in *Genealogical Research in Nova Scotia* (Halifax: 1983).

In Ontario, some early municipal tax assessment or census rolls have survived, and are listed by Brenda Merriman in her third edition of *Genealogy in Ontario*, pages 160–162. The Archives of Ontario have made available, through their Inter-Institutional Loan Service, microfilms of many pre-1851 Census, Assessment and Collectors' Rolls, Voters' Lists and Other Municipal Records. Check their Web site for the most recent lists.

POLL BOOKS AND ELECTORAL LISTS

In the mid-nineteenth century, poll books or electoral lists provided the names of property owners who had a vote. These may turn up in district, county or even township records at the appropriate provincial archive. For 1935 and after, the Records of the Chief Electoral Officer for Canada (RG 113) at the LAC include lists of voters prepared for each federal election. You must know the address or electoral district to obtain the correct microfilm.

MILITIA LISTS

Militia lists are yet another source that will place all males of fighting age in a given place at a given time, because, with a few exceptions, all able-bodied men had to serve in the militia. The initial dates depend on when the colony began and, although the militia declined after the War of 1812, the militia did not officially cease to be until the passage of the Militia Act in 1904.

A number of such lists survive in the Maritime provinces, and for Ontario *Men of Upper Canada: Militia Nominal Rolls, 1828–1829* lists and locates some 27,000 males from age 19 to 39 for a period when census and tax records are very few.[5] Some almanacs list the officers of the provincial militias, but not the other ranks.

OTHER OFFICIAL NAME LISTS

The Archives of Canada holds an indexed series of Marriage Bonds for both Upper and Lower Canada that name many early settlers, both the couple planning to marry and the two citizens who signed the bond. A similar group of unindexed bonds is held by the Archives of Nova Scotia.

In New Brunswick, county marriage registers were kept from quite early times, based on returns sent in by the various clergy. Many of the early books are in print, and the originals can be viewed on microfilm. Many publications are listed in the Information Sheet section of *Generations*, the quarterly of the New Brunswick Genealogical Society. The Archives of New Brunswick issue information sheets for each county indicating what records survive, with microfilm numbers.

For Quebec, remember that the religious institutions kept all vital records until the mid-twentieth century, depositing an annual copy with the regional Prothonotary court. While this material is rarely in "name list" form, much has been indexed in the local and regional "Indexes to ..." or "Répertoires des..." that are noted in chapter six

In Ontario, most records of marriages up to 1869 are in print. The Ontario Genealogical Society has published a wide variety of early name lists related to naturalization, emigration and probate.

In western Canada the provincial genealogical societies have ongoing indexing programs. A few are mentioned in chapter six but, with your librarian's help, and the inter-institutional loan program, you should be able to find and borrow most of what exists for your part of Canada. As well, check the Internet (see chapter six).

"PASSENGER LISTS"

Tracing Your Ancestors in Canada explains the Archives' holdings of these official lists of names that are, properly, passenger manifests; that is, lists of passengers arriving in Canadian ports. Because those from 1869 to 1919 are unindexed and 1919 to 1924 are arranged only semi-alphabetically, luck plays a large part in your search. The more you know about these lists, the better your luck. Jim Shearon clearly explained how to use the indexed and semi-indexed 1919 to 1935 records in "Using Ships' Passenger Lists to Find Records of Your Ancestors."[6]

If your ancestors arrived between 1869 and 1919, the search is more difficult. Sheila Powell's article "All Present and Accounted For" in the NAC's *The Archivist* (July-August 1990) explains the policies that produced them. You can borrow the individual microfilms, but there are additional finding aids available at the Archives that simplify the task a little. There are ring binders with yearly lists of each ship (with sailing and arrival dates) on each film for each port.

Some of this information has been extracted and made into a database available on a CD-ROM, *Passenger Ship Arrivals: Canadian Ports 1865–1899* issued by The Ships List-Research Inc. <www.theshipslist.com>. You can search by year using Departure Port, Arrival Port, Ship Name or Shipping Line to find the number of the microfilm reel. Some additional information is sometimes available but *not* passengers' names. This information could prove helpful if you plan to order the microfilms for use in your own library.

The majority of immigrants from Europe and the British Isles arrived either at Quebec City or Halifax. The number of ships arriving at Halifax is smaller than at Quebec City, but the port was open all year and the ships were larger. Many travelled on to New York or Portland, Maine, which had a direct train service to Montreal.

A few landed at Saint John, New Brunswick, but many landed at U.S. ports because of the shorter train journey to inland points. The LAC has filmed the lists of passengers destined for Canada who landed at Boston, Baltimore, New York, Portland, Philadelphia and Rhode Island for the years 1905 to 1919 or 1921 depending on the port. However, these U.S. lists include only the passengers who told the purser (who made out the lists) that they were proceeding directly to Canada.

The manifests contain much genealogical material: name, age, occupation, intended destination and some give place of birth. But individual pursers had their own ways of keeping these lists. Country of birth entries are not always geographic, some are ethnic identifications. Some pursers would put down England under country or county of birth; others put down the county in the U.K.; some list surname first, some the given name; some used stamps, some didn't. Some (of blessed memory) made their lists alphabetical — most did not.

Passenger manifest searches are relatively easy, but slow, since the names are rarely listed in any order, though passengers may be grouped by nationality. Even when a specific year is known, search time can still vary widely, it will depend on several factors: how many vessels arrived and how many passengers and from what countries (one can skim over groups from the wrong countries) were on each. A word of warning: films are sometimes backward on the reel because a user wound it off the wrong way. The early ones are confusingly filmed, difficult to sort out and often appear to have been filmed from the back to the front of the manifest. The handwriting can be hard to read or the ink may have faded. Alas, the originals were destroyed after they were microfilmed.

Very few records have survived from before 1865. In the early nineteenth century most immigrants came from the British Isles, and so were British subjects coming to British colonies. However, an index of emigrants in the early eighteenth century has been published by the OGS: John A. Acton's *Index of Some Passengers Who Emigrated to Canada between 1817 and 1849*. This indexes lists of emigrants found in records of the British Colonial Office and, according to a LAC information sheet, List of Useful Handbooks, "is a decided improvement over our finding aid to CO 384."

1915–1932 NATURALIZATION DATABASES

Two databases, produced by the Jewish Genealogical Societies of Montreal and Ottawa, have been posted on the Canadian Genealogy Centre's Web site. These databases refer to about 200,000 who applied for and received status as naturalized Canadians from 1915 to 1932. During that period, the government of Canada published the lists of names of those naturalized subjects in the annual reports of the Secretary of State (*Sessional Papers*) and in the *Canada Gazette*. The databases make it possible to search those annual lists by name.

According to the description on the Centre's Web site:

> In 1901, there were 5.3 million Canadians, of whom only one in 20 were not "British-born," a term that included Canada, England and other countries of the British Commonwealth. By 1911, due to a wave of immigration from continental Europe and the United States, one in 10 Canadian residents were from non-Commonwealth countries.

> Many of these non-British immigrants did not speak English, and often had names that English speakers had never before encountered. As well, they often had no firm plans as to where they would make their new homes in Canada. These factors pose major problems for today's genealogical researchers trying to trace the movements of their direct ancestors and other relatives. We may know whence they came, but it's not always known what names they used, and where they went.

> The databases are one of the few Canadian genealogical resources specifically designed to benefit those researchers with roots outside of the

British Commonwealth. References located in the databases can be used to request copies of the actual naturalization records held by Citizenship and Immigration Canada.

A WORD ON INDEXES

Name lists are rarely alphabetical but, if they have been transcribed and published, you can expect either an alphabetical listing or an index. If you have narrowed your search down to two or three areas where people with your family's names lived, indexes, in particular census indexes, might help you place them. The Archives Genealogy Desk keeps a list of "Indexes to Census Returns" that is regularly updated.

In Ontario the OGS *Index to the 1871 Census of Ontario* covers the entire province and is searchable on the Internet — but it lists only heads of household and strays, not entire families. Except for the LDS's complete 1881 census, most are very localized, but there are quantities of them for all parts of the country. Many indexes are prepared and published by provincial genealogical societies, or their local branches; check their lists of publications. As well, search your library catalogues for indexes made by independent individuals or groups. In New Brunswick, the NBGS's *Generations* lists a number of indexes prepared and sold by members, and most society magazines print lists for their regions.

WARNING: People make name lists and indexes and people can make mistakes — it's called human error.

$ *[illegible]*

August 1st 1895.

[handwritten: History]

[illegible] agree to take one volume of the book entitled **"Public Men of Compton County,"** to be published by L. S. Channell, Cookshire, containing a short history of the County with its towns and villages up to date, and engravings of the principal men and places.

[illegible] agree to pay for the above on delivery *Nineteen* dollars, being entitled to *half* page with engraving, the expense for necessary suitable photograph to be borne by the publisher. Copy of matter to be inserted given herewith.

Publisher reserves the right to cancel this contract if sufficient subscribers are not secured to warrant the expense of publishing.

Alonzo Todd

No alterations of this contract, or verbal agreement contrary to it, will be accepted by the publisher.

P. O. Address, *[illegible]*

Not all those who subscribed to entries in a Who's Who were prominent city-dwellers. This entry is for Alonzo Todd, a prosperous farmer, whose earlier listing in the Historical Atlas of Quebec Eastern Townships *can be found on page 68.*

CHAPTER SEVEN

Who's Who

*"Again we remind all those interested in dependable Who's Who reference, that we have never requested or received payment of any kind whatsoever to secure inclusion or exclusion."**

Somewhere between alphabetical indexes and official name lists lurk the brief biographies published in dictionary form or in local histories or atlases. In nineteenth and early twentieth-century publications, the information was usually provided by the individual being celebrated, and may well have involved a paid subscription for the book. Most of the modern directories of this or that profession ask entrants to fill out a form and accept pretty well whatever is sent to them. Standard reference works, however, like the *Dictionary of … Biography* or *Who's Who in …*, serve a wide group of users in the various media who, these days, demand accurate information and the correct facts. My advice is to be very suspicious of the past and double check the present, but never overlook such books.

BIOGRAPHICAL DICTIONARIES

Those *Prominent Men of …* publications, like early business directories and the many historical atlases, were usually published by subscription, so their coverage is restricted. Nevertheless, books like the 1888 *A Cyclopaedia of Canadian Bi-*

---

* "Notice," *The Canadian Who's Who* with which is incorporated "Canadian Men and Women of the Time"; a Biographical Dictionary of Notable Living Men and Women, Vol. VI, 1952–1954, founded and first published 1910 (Toronto: Trans Canada Press), p. ii.

ography being Chiefly Men of the Times[1] or *Prominent People of the Maritime Provinces* (1922 and 1938)[2] and all the annual editions of *The Canadian Who's Who* and its variants can be a useful source because they usually give the place of birth, names of parents and, often, earlier lineage, as well as marriage, wife, children and education. Such information can lead you to other directories, both of places and professions.

"But my ancestors were farmers, they won't be there." Don't be so sure. You would be surprised at how many Canadian farm families of modest means produced at least one noted clergyman or educator, politician or military man. The prominent Same Name may be grandad's second cousin, but such books offer good clues as to where in the country or province your family name can be found. Someone who made the *Who's Who* about 1950 was probably born around 1900 and his parents before 1875. An entry in the 1888 *Cyclopaedia* might take you back to 1800 or earlier.

The facsimile edition (1972) of Belden's 1881 *Historical Atlas of Quebec Eastern Townships*[3] includes a biographical Index of Subscribers, and here I found the birthplace, in Ontario, of a clergyman I was searching for but who had died before the publication of *Men of Today in the Eastern Townships 1917*.[4] As for this small book, it contains biographical sketches of some 1,200 prominent men, both French- and English-speaking, with considerable information on their ancestry, as well as their mothers, wives and daughters, though no women have their own entries. By 1922 when *Prominent People of the Maritimes* was published, women, though not yet legally "persons," were allotted some twenty entries. Similar books exist for all parts of Canada. Don't overlook them, they are usually all in a row on the reference shelves in the library. For example, the OGS sponsored and B & C List published *Who's Who in Ontario:*

A biographical record of men and women of our time 1995–1999.

The first edition of *The Social Register of Canada* was issued in 1958, the third in 1961, after which publication ceased.[5] A sort of social Who's Who, without a full biography, the entries give only name and address, sometimes a wife's birth name, perhaps children and, often, telephone number. Listed by province, then by major cities, with a "non-metropolitan" section, entries can be interesting if you know the community.

Always Check Local Histories

If you can link your family name to a place, check various library catalogues for any local or regional (township, village, church or county) histories that may have been published. While some histories are badly organized, unindexed, anecdotal rambles around the town, others are well-researched, -documented and -indexed, and you might find that your work has already been done. One modern Ontario township history I used gave family details of every owner of each lot or part of a lot. Older histories often exist in facsimile, like L.S. Channell's *History of Compton County and Sketches of the Eastern Townships, District of St. Francis and Sherbrooke County*, first published in 1896. Recently issued by Global Press,[6] it contains not only many biographies, but pictures of homes. My husband's great grandfather, who, by the way was a farmer, is in it; he had signed an agreement to pay 13 dollars for his copy, "being entitled to half page with engraving, the expense for necessary suitable photograph to be born by the publisher."

The Atlantic provinces are so well served by local historians that bibliographers seem unable to keep up with the authors. There are histories of most Nova Scotia counties, many also available in facsimile, but in New Brunswick it is the city or tains, 1812. Address, 92 St. Hubert Street.

Trotter, Wallace C., warehouseman and Custom House and forwarding agent. Warehouse and office, 25 Normand Street, Box 1747, Post Office.

CHAMBLY BASIN.

Martel, M. D. S., physician and surgeon. Was an M.P.P. Born in 1838, at Verchères.

LONGUEUIL.

Duprat, Rev. J. E., R. C. clergyman, and curé of Chambly. Born in L'Assomption Co., 1836.

County of Compton.

TOWNSHIP OF BURY.

Delaney, L. N., proprietor of British American Hotel, Robinson, Lower Village ; also carries on a saddlery business. Has lived in the county since 1871. Born in Richmond Co., 1850.

Lockett, Edmund, merchant and land agent, Robinson. Came to the county in 1860. Was born in London, England, 1840.

Munro, T. B., general merchant. Commenced business here in 1877. Born in Scotland, 1848. Residence and P.O. address, Robinson.

Patton, Charles, Crown Land Agent, and Secretary-Treasurer of the Municipality and School Commission. Born at Kingston, Ont., 1824. Settled here in 1852. Residence and P. O. address, Robinson.

Pope, F. M., land and lumber dealer. He holds the offices of Municipal Councillor and Chairman of the School Commission. Is also a Lieutenant-Colonel of the Volunteer Militia. Born here in 1849. Residence and P. O. address, Robinson.

TOWNSHIP OF CLIFTON.

Marshall, William, farmer and carpenter. He owns 95 acres of Lots 10 and 11, Con. 11. Settled in the county in 1858. Born in New Hampshire, 1819. P.O. address, Moe's River.

Macaulay, Major M. B., railroad contractor and lumber dealer. He owns about 300 acres in Winslow and Whitton Townships. Has lived in the county since 1852. Residence and P.O. address, Martinville.

TOWNSHIP OF EATON.

Armstrong, Robert, general merchant and Postmaster at Birchton ; is also traveller for Mathewson & Patton, of Montreal. He owns a store and 10 acres in the village. Born in Durham County, 1845. Settled here in 1880.

Alger, W. E. Owns a grist and saw mill at Johnville, also 30 acres situated on Lots 27 and 28, Con. 2. Was born in the township in 1829. P.O. address, Johnville.

Baker, E. S., Bailiff of the Superior Court, Crier of the County Court, Secretary-Treasurer of Cookshire and Township of Eaton, and also of the School Board. He was born in County Limerick, Ireland, in 1838. Settled here in 1863. Residence and P.O. address, Cookshire.

sioner for the Superior Court, and Dep. Registrar for Compton Co. Came here in 1868. Born in Bagot County, 1844. Residence and P.O. address, Cookshire.

Orr, Elias S., County Registrar since 1869, and was in business as a general merchant from 1860 to 1868. He owns 250 acres in Lots 3, 4 and 11, Cons. 3 and 8 of the township. Born in Argenteuil Co., in 1829. Came here in 1860. Residence and P. O. address, Cookshire.

Osgood, J. F., of the firm of McNicol & Osgood, general merchants, Cookshire. He is also owner of 340 acres of land in the township. Born in Compton Co., 1822. P.O. address, Cookshire.

Powers, G. W., M.D., physician and surgeon, locating here in 1862. He graduated at Vermont University in 1855, and McGill College, Montreal, in 1860. He owns 358 acres in Lots 6, 7, 8, 9 and 12, of Cons. 2, 3, 4 and 5. Born in Vermont State, in 1831. Residence and P.O. address, Eaton.

Pope, J. C., farmer. Owns 116 acres in Lots 11 and 12, Cons. 7 and 8. Is agent for the Massey Manufacturing Co., of Toronto, agricultural implement makers. Born in Cookshire, 1856. Residence and address, Cookshire.

Pope, R. H., farmer. He owns about 400 acres in Lots 11, 12, 13, 14 and 15, Cons. 7, 8 and 9, and was born in the township in 1857. Residence and P.O. address, Cookshire.

Lebourveau, M., general merchant, and Postmaster of Eaton. He also holds the offices of Mayor of the municipality and Warden of the county. Was born in Eaton in 1817.

Sawyer, William, M.P.P., proprietor of grist and saw mills at Sawyerville. He has held the offices of Mayor, Warden, &c., and was elected M.P.P. in 1871. He is still the representative. Born in the township in 1815. P.O. address, Sawyerville.

Taylor, Alexander, proprietor of Eastern Townships Hotel and Livery, at Eaton Village, since 1878 ; and was born in the county in 1846.

Todd, Alonzo, farmer. Is owner of 236 acres in Lots 12, 13 and 14, Con. 6. He has lived in the county since 1834 ; and was born in that year. P.O. address, Birchton.

Taylor, H. E., farmer and horse dealer. He owns 160 acres, and resides on Lot 7, Con. 6. Born in Compton County in 1844. P.O. address, Sawyerville.

Trigge, Mrs. Elizabeth, resides in Cookshire, and came to the county in 1843. Was born in Kent County, England.

Taylor, J. H., farmer and merchant. He owns 277 acres in Lots 13 and 16, Cons 7 and 8. Has been in the Council. Is Lieutenant-Colonel of the 5th Cavalry Regiment, a position he has held since 1873. Born in Eaton, Compton County. P.O. address, Cookshire.

Taylor, J. L., farmer. Owns 300 acres in Lots 14 and 15, Con. 5, and is an ex-Councillor. Born in Cookshire, 1830. P.O. address, Birchton.

TOWNSHIP OF NEWPORT.

Annable, L. H., M.D., physician and surgeon. Commenced practice here in 1878. Graduated in Vermont, 1865 Was born in Compton Co., 1837. Residence and P.O. address, Sawyerville.

Hurd, G. G., farmer and stockbreeder, residing on Lots 6 and 7, Con. 10, and owning 260 acres. Has been Mayor of the Municipality, and is now a Councillor. Has lived in the township since 1839. P. O. address, Sawyerville.

from Historical Atlas of Quebec Eastern Townships Illustrated, *H. Belden & Co. 1884 (reprint editor Ross Cumming, OwenSound, ON: Richardson, Bond & Wright, 1972) part of page 87 "Biographical Directory of Subscribers in the Eastern Townships and South-western Quebec." Note Alonzo Todd is in the middle column.*

town histories you should search out. Quebec, of course, has a language divide, but in English you should be able to find accounts of most Eastern Township counties as well as parts of the Outaouais.

For Ontario there are four bibliographies: William F.F. Morley's *Ontario and the Canadian North. Vol.3: Canadian local histories to 1950: a bibliography*[7] and Barbara B. Aitken's *Local Histories of Ontario Municipalities 1951–1977: A Bibliography*, with supplements covering 1977–1987 and 1987–1997.[8]

AND MAPS

This is also the point to check large-scale nineteenth-century maps. *County Atlases of Canada: a Descriptive Catalogue*[9] lists most of the nineteenth-century county atlases (most are available in facsimile, but LAC has originals as well). LAC also hold most of the huge wall maps made from 1870 to 1880.[10] Consult these on microfiche, from which prints can be made. With either atlas or map you can locate each farm lot and usually read the names of the owners. Often a local museum or library will have one or the other for your region.

As well, most of the historical atlases have short histories of each township written at a time when people still remembered the first European settlers in many districts. Some may even show Native reserves and land allotments with the names of owners. They can be very informative. Local genealogical societies have been indexing many of these so do check to see if your county atlas has been indexed.

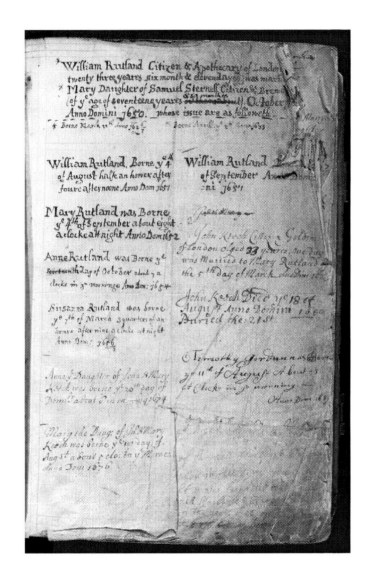

Recorded on the flyleaves of this family Bible donated to the OGS and currently in the Thomas Fisher Rare Book Library of the University of Toronto are the births, baptisms, marriages and deaths of several generations of the Rutland, Jordan, Starlinge and Yonge* families beginning here with the marriage of William Rutland to Mary Sternell on 2 October 1650. [*No link yet established to Sir George Yonge.]

CHAPTER EIGHT

Church or Census or What?

*"There are circumstances when even primary sources can be erroneous. …
the genealogical sleuth asks: is it necessarily true? Can I determine the
truth by gathering information from other sources?"**

Official registration of vital statistics came late to the British
colonies that became Canada. The genealogists' primary
source of such information remains surviving Church registers or family Bibles.

FAMILY BIBLES CAN BE WRONG

If there is a Bible, and if someone wrote down the births,
marriages and deaths, *eureka*! you have all your facts. Or do
you? First, check the date of publication. The Bible may
have been published some years *after* the dates of the first
entries. Such entries may have been copied (or miscopied)
into the new Bible from some other source. Be suspicious if
the entries are all in the same ink. The handwriting may be
the same but different inks indicate different times of writing and so are more likely to be contemporary with the event
recorded. There is a Bible in my family, published some years
after the dates of the first entries, one of which gives a marriage date that does not agree with the parish register. Count-
ing to nine explains why it was changed.

---

* Brenda Dougall Merriman, *About Genealogical Standards of Evidence: A Guide
for Genealogists* (Toronto OGS, 1997), p. 17.

WHERE IS THE PARISH REGISTER?

> Methodist records are in the United Church Archives, Presbyterian registers may be there or with the Presbyterian Archives, and if the family said they were Episcopalian check both the Church of England and Methodist Episcopal records. Church of England Parish Registers are kept by the individual Anglican Diocese Archives; those of the Roman Catholic church are also with their Diocese, but the Diocesan boundaries of the two denominations are different.[1]

Confusing? Yes. When you turn to the census in hopes of finding out what your family's religion was, and so where to look for surviving registers, you are faced with a tangled web of terminology, difficult for Canadians and worse for others. Because settlers came here from the United States as well as Great Britain, our Christian institutions evolved from both British and American churches and sects. Thus two different branches of the same denomination might be rivals in some communities, and throughout the nineteenth century they might have merged, split or changed in other ways.

For family historians it helps to have some knowledge of how the Christian denominations organize their churches, the lines of authority and, consequently, what their archives might hold. There are two basic forms: hierarchical and congregational. Hierarchical denominations, like the Roman Catholic and Anglican (Episcopalian) churches, view authority as descending from heaven to the Pope or the Crown, thence to archbishops (archdiocese), then bishops (diocese) and so down to parishes and individual parish priests, rectors or vicars. Such a structure can manage a worldwide organization with many sub-structures (such as religious orders that teach or provide for medical or social needs). Its nature is authoritarian, but it has the great advantage of keeping excellent and continuous records — at least where fire, moisture, mice and men have not been too active.

Non-conformists, the rebels against these established churches, tended to form congregational structures in which each congregation is responsible for its own activities but comes together with others in some sort of co-operative group (conference, synod or council) to manage affairs that go beyond the small unit. These structures have a tendency to split over minor points of theology and go off in all directions; their history is sprinkled with charismatic preachers and leaders. Their records, alas, are only as good as the individual sect, minister or congregation wanted them to be.

RELIGION AND THE CENSUS

The Historical Atlas of Canada sorts out the religious tangle. Volume III, Plate 34, "Religious Adherence" uses both multi-colour maps and pie-charts to display religious diversity throughout the country. It includes "The Road to Church Union," a family tree of the United Church of Canada that gives some idea of the many Protestant sects that amalgamated into one church in 1925. A similar chart is found in the *Guide to Family History Research in the Archival Repositories of the United Church of Canada*, which also discusses later expansion of membership.

The data used in the Atlas are taken from the relevant Canadian census returns where, unlike the United States, a column for "religion" was a standard element. This is useful for family historians, but the somewhat cryptic abbreviations for the many nineteenth-century denominations you find on a census return can be puzzling. If you use the Internet, go to the Archives of Canada's Web site <www.archives.ca>

and, under Genealogy Research, consult the section on Census Records. This has a list of abbreviations as well as all sorts of other information.

If you prefer your information in book form, Brenda Merriman gives a basic list on page 88 of *Genealogy in Ontario*, revised third edition, and directs researchers to the Index to the 1871 Census of Ontario for a longer list. As well, the Introduction to the *Catalogue of Census Returns on Microfilm ... 1666-1891* contains a list of abbreviations on page xii. along with a concise explanation of the census schedules.

THE ESTABLISHED CHURCHES

R.C. is obviously Roman Catholic, C. of E. the Church of England (Anglican), though I found a French-speaking census enumerator who wrote down "Englican." Expect to find Roman Catholic families in the records of the local parish or, if in remote settlements, in the records of various missions at the diocese headquarters. Anglican parish records are also kept by the diocese, though again, various missionaries sent out by the Society for the Propagation of the Gospel or others may have baptised whole families in some remote areas. In the *Directory of Canadian Archives* there are addresses for the various Anglican diocesan archives and Roman Catholic archdiocese, diocese and some parochial archives, as well as those of many Roman Catholic religious orders. In some jurisdictions you may require the permission of the bishop or archbishop before you can use the records, even if the microfilms are held in the provincial archives.

Many records are only available through the church. You will find some diocesan archives are very helpful; others are quite uninterested in assisting genealogists. Most have to charge for services these days, but if they do not, try to make a contribution to further their work.

THE NON-CONFORMISTS

By 1891 most non-conformists had a family church and clergyman but, in the early years of the colonies, settlers themselves were inconsistent, often because their denomination had no church or clergy in an area. In the *Historical Atlas of Canada*, Plate 34, G.J. Matthews' pedigree chart "The Road to Church Union" shows clearly how many local and regional Presbyterian synods had to join together to form the Presbyterian Church in Canada (1867), and is equally enlightening as to when and how Wesleyan Methodists, Methodist Episcopal Churches (American and Canadian), Primitive Methodists, Bible Christians and New Connexion Methodists slowly got together by 1884 to become the Methodist Church of Canada, Newfoundland & Bermuda.

Pres. is Presbyterian (a member of a church governed by elders all of equal rank), a definition that applies to those labelled C. of S. (Church of Scotland or the Kirk), but not to the Episcopal Church in Scotland. F.C. or P.F.C. is the Presbyterian Free Church, R.P. Reformed Presbyterian, U.P. United Presbyterian. Cameronians are a small group that broke from the Church of Scotland and were active in early Eastern Ontario settlements.

If early Presbyterian congregations were schism-prone, so were their Methodist neighbours, who may appear as M. or Meth. or as Wes., W.M., or Wesleyans. E.M. means Episcopal Methodists, Baptists are usually shown as Bp. or Bap., Quakers as Q. Universalists, Bible Christians (B.C.), and other less familiar sects are generally written out. Every now and then some individualist says "None."

Baptist, and in early days in Nova Scotia, Newlight Baptist, congregations had "an historic theological bias against record keeping" and as Phillip G.A. Griffin-Allwood explains, do not expect to find birth dates since "Baptists practice [adult] believer's baptism."[2] Moreover, you must know which denomination of Baptist your ancestors were. For example, were they Regular Baptists or Particular Dependent Closed Communion Baptists or some other branch of the Baptist Church?

People who may or may not be of the Jewish faith are variously recorded as Jew, Jewish, Hebrew, Israelite, the French equivalents of all four or Jewish Church [sic] under religion. Jew, Jewish or Hebrew also appears under origin, alone or modifying the country of origin.[3]

In Quebec, where religious institutions were responsible until very recently for all recording of vital statistics, Unitarian ministers sometimes obliged those with no religious affiliations, particularly for marriages.

THE UNITED CHURCH OF CANADA

The United Church of Canada is an institution unique to Canada with which researchers from other countries may not be familiar. On 10 June 1925, Church Union amalgamated the Methodist Church of Canada, about half the Presbyterians, the Congregational Union and the Union Churches of Western Canada into the United Church of Canada. Since the United Church absorbed all the Methodist and Congregational churches in Canada, it holds whatever earlier records survive from these two groups. However, not all Presbyterians joined so their records are divided between the United Church Archives and those of the Presbyterian Church of Canada.

CHURCH ARCHIVES

Like all things Canadian, church records and those who hold them, are divided regionally, not so much by province as by early church districts. The principal Archives of the United Church of Canada are located at Victoria University, a part of the University of Toronto, but there are also six regional Conference Archives, and some material is held at various universities, like Mount Allison in Sackville, New Brunswick, that were founded originally as denominational colleges.[4] The same holds true for the Baptists. The Canadian Baptist Archives are at McMaster Divinity College in Hamilton, Ontario, but Acadia University Archives in Wolfville, Nova Scotia holds the historic records of the Baptist Church in Atlantic Canada.

There are some useful published sources that can help you find your way through the mysteries of religious denominations. The *Directory of Canadian Archives* (1990) lists most church and denominational archives and gives some idea of their holdings. For the addresses of religious archives look in the index that groups archives by category, under "Religion." The Lutheran and Mennonite Church's archives, the Salvation Army and the Canadian Jewish Congress National Archives are included. But there is nothing to tell you that the Society of Friends (Quakers) holdings are at Pickering College in Newmarket, Ontario, much less that they are extensive and available on microfilm at the Archives of Ontario and Library and Archives Canada.[5] The Directory has not been reprinted since, but most of the information is now available on the Internet.

Most libraries will have the six volumes of *The Encyclopedia of Canada*, but probably in the stacks. Edited by the noted historian W. Stewart Wallace it was published by University Associates Canada in three different editions: the first in 1935–37, a registered edition in 1940 and the second in 1948. This is worth hunting down; in the twenty-first century it is an invaluable guide to the recent past. It contains useful brief histories of the major Christian denominations and many individual Religious Orders (look under Sisters, Brothers, Jesuits, etc.). It also has entries for communities across the country that list which railways served them, what newspapers were published and what industries were important before World War II.

Archivaria is the journal of the Association of Canadian Archivists, published semi-annually. No. 30 (summer 1990)is devoted largely to Canadian religious archives and, between the various articles, Notes and Communications and the book reviews provides an overview of less well-known archival activities. For example, it includes a description of the project that produced the *Guide to the Records of the Canadian Unitarian and Universalist Churches, Fellowships, and Other Related Organizations*, compiled by Heather M. Watts (Halifax, 1990).

Archivaria, no.31 (winter 1990–91) describes "Mennonite Archives in Canada" and you will also find a review of *Records of the Anglican Church of Canada. Volume 2: Guide to the Holdings of the Ecclesiastical Province of Ontario.* A joint effort of the archivists of this ecclesiastical administrative unit, it is the second volume in a series that originated in 1986 with *Guide to the Holdings of the Archives of Rupert's Land.* The *Guide to the Holdings of the Ecclesiastical Province of British Columbia and the Yukon* was published in 1993.

A stone in the pioneer cemetery, Dorchester, N.B. transcribed in 1975 when it was whole. By 1990 it lay on the ground in pieces.

CHAPTER NINE

In Loving Memory Of …

*"And the grave's the place to seek them."**

In the chill of autumn, the wet of spring or the heat of summer, dedicated genealogists get down on their knees and push aside prickly shrubs, pull up grass and scrape away moss or even earth to decipher and transcribe the inscriptions on gravestones.

   Stone is not forever, especially inscriptions carved in stone. Weather and erosion, neglect and vandals, new roads and housing developments conspire to destroy this legacy from our past. As family historians we can only be grateful and support the work of the many local historical and genealogical societies that have persevered and are still struggling to preserve the information on these memorials. Such work is almost always a local or even an individual effort, and there are so many tiny, rural burial sites and so many huge urban ones that to list what is available throughout Canada's ten provinces and three territories would fill this book ten times.

START AT THE PROVINCIAL LEVEL

The search starts at the provincial level. Although the work is local, in recent times most cemetery or epitaph projects have been coordinated through provincial genealogy socie-

* Robert Louis Stevenson, "In Scots," XVI, Stanza 3, *Underwoods*.

ties. A list of addresses begins on page 103. Using a library's computerized catalogue, start searching under Subject: Cemeteries — province — place, or try Registers of births etc. — province — place, these should bring up holdings of published transcripts.

For Ontario, where one of the most extensive projects is underway, the Ontario Genealogical Society's *Publications for Sale 1998*, lists publications of all their branches, including the many cemetery indexes and cemetery transcriptions available. Of course more has been done in the past few years and more will be done, so a check of regional society Web sites should turn up further efforts.

Large metropolitan centres like Montreal and Toronto are made up of many small communities that have grown together, so you must expect to find many small, older burial grounds tucked away in older churchyards. The Toronto Branch OGS published a *Directory of the Cemeteries in the Municipality of Metropolitan Toronto and Regional Municipality of York* in 1989,[1] tracking down over 300 graveyards and indicating which had been transcribed. This branch has also established a consolidated computerized index to these transcripts that is updated regularly.

The Quebec Family History Society, Pointe Claire sells a bulletin *The LOCATION of CEMETERY GRAVE LISTS In and Near the Province of QUEBEC* that lists known transcripts and where they are located. Many are held in the society library and you should write to them directly for the price and availability of the latest issue.

The graveyards in tiny Prince Edward Island are almost all transcribed. In 1991 over three hundred published lists were available from the provincial genealogical society. The other Atlantic provinces are less well-served. Newfoundland and Labrador has started a transcription project, as has New Brunswick, but in both, as well as Nova Scotia, there is a need to coordinate work done in the early part of the twentieth century with more current efforts.

In the 1990s serious work was done in both Moncton and Saint John, New Brunswick, and is now in print. For other areas you must check with local historical or genealogical society branches.

Manitoba, Saskatchewan, Alberta, British Columbia and Yukon Territory all have projects well underway, and lists of publications are constantly updated. Again, write the provincial society, or check their Web sites, for the latest publication lists.

On the Internet

You can search databases for Ontario and British Columbia on the Internet. The Ontario Cemetery Finding Aid, a pointer database or "finding aid," is at <www.islandnet.com/ocfa/homepage.html>. Its purpose is to "point" you to, or help you "find," the location of more information. This is usually the published transcripts that small regional societies sell to support their work. The transcripts consist of the surnames, cemetery name and location of over two million interments from several thousand cemeteries, cairns, memorials and cenotaphs in Ontario, Canada. The file does not contain transcriptions or dates, but it does tell the reader which county, township and cemetery contains a given surname. The researcher can then obtain the complete transcript for that particular cemetery from the contributing organizations. An address page lists where to purchase the transcripts.

Currently, the complete OCFA '98,' versions 5 and 6 combined (two million names) can be searched on their Web site. A listing of the cemeteries that are included is sorted by county in the Cemetery List pages.

Another Cemetery Finding Aid from the author of OCFA is the British Columbia Cemetery Finding Aid

<www.islandnet.com/bccfa/>. Version 2 contains over 340,000 entries. Again it is a pointer database consisting of the surnames, cemetery names and location, collected from records and headstone inscriptions associated with 264 cemeteries in British Columbia, Canada, and two from the state of Washington, USA. This version includes all previous BCCFA entries.

There is also a link to the very useful Canadian genealogy site, Canadian Genealogy and History Links <www.islandnet.com/~ jveinot/cghl/cghl.html>.

OUR CRUMBLING PAST

Because wood and stone are so perishable, it is always a good idea to check whether work done by earlier generations of antiquarians and local historians is held at provincial archives, regional libraries or museums. Often a manuscript or typescript copy was deposited in a local institution and librarians and curators will know if local material has been published. For example, William Inglis Morse's *Gravestones of Acadie* and his *The Land of the New Adventure: The Georgian Era in Nova Scotia*,[2] both of which include many photographs and transcripts of inscriptions of early Nova Scotia gravestones made almost a century ago. One summer in Halifax I picked up a small book: *Life how short Eternity how long — Gravestone Carving and Carvers in Nova Scotia*.[3] It too is lavishly illustrated with many photographs of eighteenth-century gravestones, and serves to remind us never to overlook the art and artifact section of any library or book store.

Always ask at local museums or libraries if such volumes exist for the region. These repositories usually have copies and may even hold the original manuscripts of such efforts. Who knows, there might be a cache of unpublished photographs, or extra pages of transcripts. This is particularly important for the long-settled Maritime provinces where the grave markers are older and often made of a local sandstone whose surface layer tends to flake off and takes the inscription with it. Work done a century ago cannot be checked today, much less repeated, unless someone took a picture. Indeed, stones I transcribed and photographed thirty-some years ago for my own files are now little more than blocks of sand.

CEMETERY RECORDS

A second type of information is found in burial registers or cemetery records maintained by local burial grounds. In the larger cities these are sometimes available, even computerized, but you must know which cemetery and be quite precise as to names and dates. In Montreal, for example, though records for the huge cemetery complex on Mount Royal are computerized, they are divided by denomination: Cimetière Nôtre-Dame-des-Neiges (Roman Catholic) and Mount Royal Cemetery for all the "Others" (including a Jewish section). The separate cemetery offices will search for one or two names but charge a small amount for further searches. Both have Web sites.

However, these are not the only cemeteries on the Island of Montreal. Like the Toronto region, many small communities have grown together and there are cemeteries in the west-island suburbs as well as in the eastern end, and in Laval there is the large St-Laurent Roman Catholic cemetery, whose office also responds to queries.

In Ottawa, Beechwood Cemetery *Burial Records ... 1873–1900* and the *Interment Registry Index 1901–1930* and *1931–1955* have been published by the local OGS Branch, and are now available on CD.[4]

FUNERAL HOMES

A third form of burial data is found in the records of undertakers and funeral homes. Sometimes, when older businesses close down, their records are placed in a local library or museum. Locating such holdings usually involves writing to each institution, though local genealogical society branches can probably help with names and addresses. Some may even be at the LAC. For example, Benjamin's, a long-established funeral home serving the Toronto Jewish community deposited its unindexed, pre-1964 record books at the LAC.

If your local university or reference library happens to have a copy of the *Union List of Manuscripts in Canadian Repositories* it is worth looking under the name of the community. A single volume was published in 1968 by the Public Archives of Canada. A more extensive, three-volume edition, with supplements, superseded it and now Archives Canada, on the Internet, offers the same sort of information (see page 19).

OBITUARIES

A date on a gravestone may or may not be correct, so do not rest content with the name and date these provide. Wherever possible follow them back to newspapers. If at all possible, try to find the obituary. For example, if your ancestor died anywhere in the Eastern Townships of Quebec, the *Sherbrooke Record* is noted for its long, informative obituaries. Mind you, it sometimes took the stringer a month or two to compose the tribute to a local worthy, so the hunt may be a long one, but it's well worth it.

Rarer than obituaries, but sometimes found in rural papers are reports of larger funerals. These provide all sorts of family information: names of out-of-town mourners and lists of "floral tributes" can offer leads to family connections. Do read the Social Notes for a week or two after the event to see who may have come to town to attend the funeral and stayed to visit around the family.

CHAPTER TEN

Royal Gazettes and Local Luminaries

*There's "more than news in the newspaper"**

Clearing out the family's attic, I found a box of old newspapers that included one issue of the impressively titled *Dunnville Luminary, Monk County Advocate and General Advertiser*. It was Volume 2, #3 bearing the date of Friday December 4, 1868. During the latter half of the nineteenth century there were literally thousands of these small (four to eight pages) local papers, usually weeklies, published all across North America. Some have had very long lives, though often under a variety of names. Others died in infancy. Some have been saved for posterity, others are lost and forgotten or, like the *Dunville Luminary*, survive by chance.

Let us all bless the Recordak Corporation, which introduced microfilming of newspapers, because, for family historians, one of the real treasures to be found at most repositories will be a collection of regional and local newspapers, some original, but most now on microfilm. The microfilms may contain issues brought together from a number of collections into a more or less "complete run" for the researcher's convenience and delectation.

---

* Christine Rose (CG, CGL, FASG) and Kay Germain Ingalls (CGRS), *The Complete Idiot's Guide to Genealogy* (New York: Alpha Books, 1997); this quote is the title of chapter 15. While this guide is oriented to United States research, it contains many useful tips and suggestions, and chapter 15, on newspapers, is well worth reading.

DELIGHTS OF TIME TRAVEL

Yes, delectation, for there is nothing that puts you in your ancestors shoes faster than reading his or her daily or weekly newspaper. It is time travel made easy but, beware if you are actually looking for specific facts and events. You must concentrate on the task at hand and not be distracted by gossipy accounts of elopements or court cases or local feuds and scandals.

ROYAL GAZETTES

In the British Colonies that became Canada, an official government *Royal Gazette* was issued regularly almost as soon as the colony was established. Chris Raible surveys these early Royal Gazettes in "'A Printer is Indispensably Necessary': The tribulations of Canada's earliest printers."[1] Alas, the article contains a misleading error. The first Canadian newspaper, Bushell's *The Halifax Gazette*, was first published in Nova Scotia on 23 March 1752, not 1762. The *Quebec Gazette* dates from 1764, *The Royal Gazette* and *New Brunswick Advertiser*'s first extant issue is dated 11 October 1785, but *The Upper Canada Gazette or American Oracle* was not launched until April 1793. Official gazettes, under one title or another, still announce government appointments and print notices of new legislation and, until recently, were still published by the Queen's Printer.

In the early days some functioned more like newspapers, but marriage and death notices were limited to Very Important People and the best most family historians can hope for is some paid announcement about an estate. In most colonies, however, other publishers were also at work though most of the contents of these papers were reprinted from British or American sources. However, the editorial, a couple of columns of local news, some death and marriage announcements (very few births) and the local advertisements and paid notices will offer a good record of community affairs.

POLITICS MATTERED

What papers you can search will depend on what was published and which survive. The *Montreal Gazette* dates from the late 1700s and the *Montreal Herald* was founded in 1811. In those days remember that "… all the newspapers were violently partisan, and their editors and reporters, men whose pens might have been dipped in acid, so cutting were the phrases they used to describe their opponents. The *Gazette* and the *Herald* were true-blue Tories."[2]

Even a small centre might have rival papers. A lively account of one such editorial rivalry is given by John Edward Belliveau, "Hawke of the *Transcript*: A forgotten hero of Canadian journalism."[3] This was in Moncton, New Brunswick, where the evening paper, the *Transcript*, was Liberal, while the *Moncton Times*, the morning paper, was Tory [Conservative]. For your area, check in local histories. Where such rivalries existed always look through both papers. Your family may only have placed notices in the one whose politics they favoured. For help in sorting out the politics of early newspapers, see the "Journalism" entry in *The Encyclopedia of Canada*, edited by W. Stewart Wallace.[4]

There are factors to consider beyond politics. Until well into the twentieth century, larger cities in Canada normally had several daily papers; at least a morning and evening paper, often a third that came out — or arrived by train — to be sold at noon. Each paper served a different audience. When English-speaking Montreal had several daily papers and a dozen suburban weeklies, the *Gazette* was a business paper and its social notices covered the lives and interests of wealthy English-speaking "society," similar to Toronto's *Globe and Mail*. For accounts of local events, accidents or disasters, the *Montreal Star* (which also carried many more marriages and obituaries) or *La Presse* are far better sources, similar in character to the *Toronto Star*. French-speaking intellectuals are served by *Le Devoir*, a good source of political and cultural news. Similar distinctions will apply in other cities but only local experience or sensitive research will reveal them — and remember that contents and editorial views might change over half a century. In Montreal, the once true-blue Tory *Herald* was, when I knew it, a tabloid that came out in the late morning and carried little or no social news.

Most city or small town newspapers served the surrounding farming regions, often delivered by the newly built railways. By the end of the nineteenth century most local papers had "stringers" who regularly sent in social notes from villages or crossroad communities. Knowing who came to town for a wedding or a funeral can be very helpful.

THE BIG *IF*

If your ancestors lived in a region served by local newspapers, *if* an institution has kept copies, *if* publication dates and your ancestors' dates coincide and *if* you can get your hands on microfilms, you might learn all sorts of fascinating things. How do you find out what papers still exist, and where?

Go to the reference desk of the best research library in your region. Large universities or a big city's central reference library will have shelves of bibliographies and union lists. ask the librarian or, if the catalogue is now computerized, try the subject heading Canadian Newspapers. Then narrow the search to single provinces: Canadian Newspapers—Name of Province. Call up entries for Bibliography.

LIST OF CANADIAN NEWSPAPERS

The National Library of Canada once issued (on 33 microfiches) a *Union List of Canadian Newspapers* (Ottawa, 1988) that brought together bibliographical data on some 10,000 titles. It is the sort of research tool that only a librarian could love or probably explain to you. Easier to use is their hard copy *Union List of Newspapers held by Canadian Libraries*.[5] An even older source is the 1959 *Canadian Newspapers on Microfilm*[6] but the Library of Canada's Web site now includes detailed lists of all their newspaper holdings, indexes, etc., and is well worth browsing.

The Library of Canada has a very extensive newspaper collection, but other repositories have other treasures. Most university libraries have a selection of nineteenth-century newspapers on microfilm. The history department sees to this. But the dates and papers may depend on their professors' specialties, so you may find what you want in unexpected places.

J. Brian Gilchrist's *Inventory of Ontario Newspapers 1793–1986*,[7] will show what Ontario newspapers exist. For Quebec, André Beaulieu's *La presse québécoise: des origines à nos jours…* is a compilation, in French, of all Quebec-published newspapers.[8] Volumes I and II are a chronological listing from 1764. The numerous English-language newspapers that at one time abounded in the Eastern Townships as well as those of Montreal and Quebec City are included. There is also at least one published list for the other provinces and the Yukon that should give details of publication dates, changes of titles and mergers.

NEWSPAPERS HAVE FAMILY TREES

Researchers should be alert to newspapers' title changes when citing sources. The current Toronto *Globe and Mail* amalgamated George Brown's *Globe* founded in 1844, with the Toronto *Mail and Empire*. This paper in turn "... was formed in 1895 by the union of the *Mail*, founded in 1872 ... and the *Empire* founded in 1887 — the two morning newspapers which catered to the Conservative element in Toronto."[9]

This sort of amalgamation of newspapers has happened in most parts of Canada. For example, the *New Brunswick Newspaper Directory* 1996 edition's "Appendix A," titled "Publishing Histories," shows these changes and mergers in family-tree form for newspapers in every community in the province.

CURRENT PUBLICATIONS

If you want to write to a local paper, the *Canadian Serials Directory* lists periodicals and newspapers (with addresses and other contact information) that were active in 1987.[10] For currently published papers, try to find a recent copy of *Matthews List*,[11] which is brought out several times a year, listing all Canadian advertising media including newspapers.

ARE THEY INDEXED?

There is an easier way to cull information from local papers than sitting with your head in a microfilm reader. Various provincial genealogical societies or individual genealogists — may heaven reward them — have prepared indexes to vital statistics for assorted newspapers. Some have been published; some exist in manuscript form or as a card file in local libraries and archives.

The Library of Canada's updated, computerized version of their *Checklist of Indexes to Canadian Newspapers held by the National Library of Canada* is available at <www.nlc-bnc.ca>.

This is a good source of current information on the many new newspaper indexes that are being published in every province every year. The older *Checklist of Indexes to Canadian Newspapers* may also prove helpful,[12] particularly in indicating which libraries hold card-index files for local papers. A card file in Ottawa is not much use to a genealogist working in Texas but, if what you want to know is limited and you can phrase your question simply, such libraries might check their card indexes and send a brief answer. Some published indexes, however, may be available through inter-institutional loans, and others may be purchased from the compiler.

I would simply note that the best-served province is New Brunswick. Daniel F. Johnson, B.B.A., C.G.(C)'s *Vital Statistics from New Brunswick (Canada) Newspapers 1784–189+*,[13] now covers the years 1784 through 1894, but with 94 volumes as of June 2003 and more expected every year, it will help if you can limit your time block. He has ranged beyond the Births, Marriages and Death notices, to include coroners' inquests, passenger lists and accounts of Maritime sailors lost at sea. Similar indexes to newspapers exist for the other Atlantic provinces but cover shorter time spans. Information from Prince Edward Island newspapers is included in the *Master Name Index*, available on microfilm.

The past two centuries have seen so many newspapers come and go in Quebec and Ontario that a province-wide index would be an impossibility. The Ontario Genealogical Society's lists of publications for sale on each branch's Web site should indicate which branches have indexed local papers.

Periodicals published by religious denominations in Ontario are a rich source of obituary material. Some early extracts have been published by Hunterdon House: examples are *Ontario Marriage Notices* (1982); and an ongoing series of *Death Notices from the Christian Guardian*, compiled by D.A. McKenzie, as well as his *More Notices from Methodist Newspapers 1830–1857*. Hunterdon's periodical *Ontario Register* is well-indexed and includes many early newspaper notices. Moreover, it is now available as a database on CD-ROM, but requires Family Tree Maker for Windows. Look for new publications and electronic databases from this press.[14]

The LAC once had an alphabetical-by-name card index to the *Quebec Gazette*, from 1764 to 1823. This is now Finding Aid 1807 that was microfilmed in 1975 (Reels C-7071–C-7095). If you check in ArchiviaNet you will learn "The subject entries are somewhat idiosyncratic, but nonetheless extensive."

Marlene Simmons has been indexing various Quebec Eastern Township newspapers, and has published an *Index to Richford Vermont Gazette & Journal Gazette, 1880–1957*.[15] This contains many Canadian entries from across the border, a reminder that for all the border townships one should be sure to search to the south as well as north.

The Manitoba Genealogical Society in Winnipeg has an ongoing program of publishing indexes to marriage and death notices from Manitoba newspapers. The Saskatchewan Genealogical Society is indexing births, deaths and marriages from Regina newspapers, in particular the *Regina Leader Post*, while the Saskatchewan Archives Board has compiled other indexes that the Society will search for a fee. The Alberta Society is preparing an index to local archival records while the Archives of British Columbia and the Yukon Archives both have some indexes that lead to newspaper obituaries or other stories.

CHAPTER ELEVEN

Historical Atlas of Canada

*"The past is a foreign country — you need a map!"**

Maps are useful tools for genealogical research anywhere, but when your ancestors were the wandering kind, who moved across this continent always hoping to find a greener pasture, maps are indispensable.[1] If some branch of your family lived in Canada during the past three hundred years, one of the most fascinating reference works to browse through is the *Historical Atlas of Canada*, a three-volume work that surveys this half-continent from "The Beginning" to 1961.[2] However, these three volumes are more than a collection of maps — much, much more. Geoffrey J. Matthews, the cartographer and designer, has put together vast amounts of information in easily understood form, using maps, charts, drawings and graphs of all sorts. In the three volumes you will find double-page plates that will explain where people came from, where they settled, how they lived, what sort of house they lived in, what they grew or hunted or caught, the jobs they may have held, how they travelled and where they played and at what.

Volume I: From the Beginning to 1800, which came out in 1987, devotes the first 18 plates to describing the land and its peoples before the advent of Europeans. There follow plates describing European fisheries, early settlement, exploration and the fur trade, and the wars between the European powers. If someone in your family was Acadian, plate 29 shows the Acadian Marshland Settlements in great detail, with the population

Here Be Dragons, p. 65.

distribution from 1671 to 1714. Plate 31 explains the origins in both old and New England of the pre-Revolutionary English-speaking settlers of Nova Scotia. American invasions of Quebec are shown in plate 44 and whole sections are devoted to the French settlements along the Saint Lawrence and to the expansion of the fur trade. Plate 62 pinpoints where every trading post was from 1774 to 1821 and plate 64 has actual floor plans of some of the trading posts and buildings.

Volume II: The Land Transformed 1800–1891, published in November 1993, spans the years of settlement and population expansion. Instead of long-winded verbal explanations of how various parts of the country were surveyed and farms laid out, this is shown in map outlines. Since they were created by computer for this volume, they easily show changes in agricultural production and the expansion of the major cities. Plate 14 is an array of maps of Ontario (Canada West) marked out in townships and showing the dates of settlement, cleared land in 1842, wheat production 1851, patterns of settlement and the layout of a typical farm. Knowing when someone came to Canada, you can easily tell where they probably found land.

Plate 24 details the "British Garrisons to 1871," showing where some army ancestor may have been posted. Plate 21 shows the many configurations of colonies, provinces and territories between 1798 and 1900. You can see at a glance where New Caledonia, the District of Assiniboia and the contested Oregon Territory once were, or study other boundary disputes that left the settlers wondering which country they lived in.

The fur trade and the fisheries were still important and, if your ancestors were involved, there is much information. Did someone take a "country wife"? Plates 32 to 35 will show you where every Native reserve is, or was, to be found and how the Métis were dispersed after the Rebellion of 1870 to 1885. Plates 25, 26 and 27 shows how railways expanded across the country and also linked Canada and the United States. Some lines were built by American firms, others by British or Scottish contractors; all brought their engineers and skilled workmen to Canada. If they included your ancestors, who may have stayed on to homestead, plate 42 will show where you might expect to find them at certain time periods. If you know they moved to "the States" between 1860 and 1900, plate 31 will show which states had the most Canadian-born residents in 1880. Many plates include pictures of typical housing styles or views from historic plates or paintings.

Volume III: Addressing the Twentieth Century 1891–1961 (1990) brings us into the twentieth century and the emphasis is more on economic growth and the expansion of industry in various places. If some members of your family were among the hundreds of thousands from the "Old World" who brought their skills to "America" via Canada, in the twentieth century, the patterns of development — be it in railways (plate 6), industry (plate 13), mining (plate 11) or farming (plates 17, 18) — may explain why they settled where they did and, perhaps, why they left. "Drought and Depression on the Prairies" in the 1920s and 1930s is demonstrated in plate 43, including the resulting out-migration.

Schooling, sports, public health, recreational land, strikes, social insurance, the post-war expansion of Metropolitan Toronto are all set out in fascinating coloured detail. The houses people lived in, the roads and rail lines they moved along, are all there to enrich your understanding of your ancestors and may explain in part why they did what they did.

Alas, while fascinating, the Atlas is not light reading. The Volumes are "atlas"-size and heavy. The price is high, though a bargain for what you get. Unless you are deeply into Canadian studies and feel you must have your own copy (as I did), look for it in larger reference libraries or university history or geography department libraries.

THE CONCISE VERSION

In 1998 a one-volume *Concise Historical Atlas of Canada* was published using plates and text from the original three-volume set, but with a thematic arrangement that groups related plates from all three.[3] For example, plate 10 "From Sea to Sea" shows territorial growth to 1900; plate 11 continues with territorial evolution from 1891 to 1961. In some ways it is easier to use; plates for the wars and invasions, settlement or transportation are brought together. Of course it only contains about one-third of the plates and the missing ones are those with all the oddball data, such as the locations of the British garrisons.

LINES OF COUNTRY

Geoffrey Matthews has brought his cartographic skills to another recent book that is very helpful in locating and tracking migrant ancestors. *Lines of Country: An Atlas of Railway and Waterway History in Canada* will show you where, and when, every rail line and waterway in Canada was built, operated and abandoned.[4] The maps are detailed, the text absolutely packed with information, the illustrations fascinating; and there is a bibliography and an index. It is about the same size as the Historical Atlas volumes, but landscape rather than portrait layout.

Knowing which railways served your ancestor's community and where they ran to may offer a clue as to where missing family members might have moved. For example, if your town was on the main CPR line from Montreal to Boston, those would be the big cities to check first, then smaller centres along the line. Perhaps a son or brother worked for "the railroad" — 90 percent of the time that would be whichever line served the home town.

CHAPTER TWELVE

Advice on Web Sites and Databases

SEARCH TOOLS

SUBJECT DIRECTORIES contain highly structured and catego-
rized lists of sites in a hierarchical arrangement easily
searched by following ordered links. Yahoo is probably the
most familiar of these, but there are others that also attempt
to index the Web.

SEARCH ENGINES, currently the best-known and popular of
which is Google, return results based on how many sites link
to the retrieved page and their popularity.

These two major types of web search tools are built
differently and should be used differently, states Marion
Press, a librarian at the Ontario Institute for Studies in
Education at the University of Toronto. She teaches a variety
of courses on the use of the Internet for genealogy, and at
OGS Seminar 2003 she made a presentation "Using the
Internet: Making Internet Search Tools Work for You," which
is outlined in the Syllabus, pages 19 to 22. The first two
pages list useful search engines and their URLs, the third
and fourth offer "Ten Steps for Improving Your Chances"
and "How to use Google Effectively."

If you do not have ready access to such help, among the
Economist Books is *Pocket Internet*, which provides a
dictionary of the arcane jargon and acronyms used on the

Internet and a potted history of how the Internet came to be and, among other "Internet tips," a page of excellent advice on "Using Search Engines" and how to conduct searches.[1]

Both stress that researchers should:

- Read the Help Screen and study how to enter search terms and, in particular, learn how to limit what is brought back to you so you are not faced with an overwhelming number of choices.

- Make your search terms as specific and unique to your subject as possible, remembering that "complete phrases in quotation marks" (or whatever protocol is used to enter a multi-word subject) will get better results than a single term.

CHANGE IS THE ONLY CONSTANT

Everyone who runs a Web site wants to improve and update it. This means that whatever is valid information on Web site addresses or search procedures today will be wrong to-morrow. Webmasters also want their sites to be different, distinctive and unique. This means that, except for clicking on underlined topic titles, no two work quite the same way. You have to guess, experiment and sometimes get lost.

1. The [← BACK] button is an essential research tool.
2. Do not feel it is beneath you to read the "Help" screen.

GOVERNMENTS LOVE IT

Governments are hooked on the Internet as the "new way to reach out to voters." Hints 1 and 2 apply to most pages. All provincial governments have Web sites where you should be able to find their Archive's page and information on how to obtain a birth certificate. However, this may depend on guessing which department or ministry handles what you want.

Finding your way around Web sites can vary widely. Some government sites need imaginative search techniques; others are easy to use. If a "Welcome" page offers a "Search" option, fill in the box with a search term such as "Archives" or "Birth Certificate" or what you want — hit the search button and you may actually reach the information page.

Hint: If your search term is more than one word, enclosing the whole term in quotation marks often will limit the search to the complete term, instead of each reference to "Birth" and each to "Certificate." Read any Help screen for ways to focus your search.

"Frequently Asked Questions" (FAQs) — if there is such a topic title — will sometimes get you to vital statistics or birth certificates. All else failing, read what the site says about various departments and their responsibilities and look for "registration," "certificates," etc.

LINKS

An easy way to access Web sites is to find a page with links to related subjects. Many pages offer some; some pages offer many:

For Archives go to: <www.usask.ca/archives/>

> Links to just about every archive in Canada, searchable by geographical region and type (provincial, municipal, university, medical, etc.).

The Canadian Genealogy Centre: <www.genealogy.gc.ca>

> This site will probably become your major source of genealogical links, but it will take time to develop.

Libraries: <www.nlc-bnc.ca>, click on Services for various menus.

> The LAC has a great collection of links to research-related and library listings under Services for Researchers, for Libraries, etc.

From these three sites, you can locate and bookmark dozens of sites with links that suite your particular interests and needs.

PROS KNOW HOW

It is great fun to surf amateur genealogists' web pages because you never know what you will find — or if it has been proofread. But you will probably find links to standard, reliable sources on the Web sites that cater to professional researchers. After all, librarians, archivists, curators and university professors have a vested interest in encouraging and maintaining sites with accurate information and links to useful data they and their colleagues may want to use. Nevertheless, for a good selection of links to genealogical and historical societies, museums and libraries in Canada, use Jessica Vienot's *Canadian Genealogy and History Links* <www.islandnet.com/~jveinot/cghl/cghl.html>

DANGER: ICEBERGS!

Databases are, essentially, electronic indexes that you can search in a variety of ways. However, no index ever picks up everything — I know, I've made indexes. What you get might be almost complete and almost error free, but only too often it is just the tip of a large iceberg. There is almost always hidden material not in the index. This can be particularly true of many database indexes you encounter on the Internet. The iceberg analogy originates with Patricia

Kennedy of the LAC whose advice in *Canadian State Trials* you were advised to read in chapter one.

Let us end as we began, with warnings:

Always Read the Fine Print and Explanations

Make sure you know exactly what has been indexed. Frequently, something is missing. Many databases were started in the 1970s or early 1980s, when computers were very big and their memories very small. Those who compiled these databases had to limit both the number of fields indexed and the size of these fields. Any database that has been around since the early 1990s is suspect; see chapter five.

Some Useful Addresses

ARCHIVES

NATIONAL
Library and Archives Canada
(LAC)
395 Wellington Street
Ottawa, ON K1A 0N3
Tel: 613-996-7458
Fax: 613-995-6274
www.archives.ca
www.nlc-bnc.ca
Produces a free booklet: *Tracing Your Ancestors in Canada*

PROVINCIAL
Provincial Archives of Alberta
12845-102 Avenue North West
Edmonton, AB T5N 0M6
Tel: 780-427-1056
Fax: 780-427-4646
www.gov.ab.ca/mcd/mhs/paa/
paa.htm

B.C. Archives
655 Belleville Street, Victoria
mailing address: Box 9419
Station Provincial Government
Victoria, BC V8V 9V1
Tel: 250-387-1952
Fax: 250-387-2072
www.bcarchives.gov.bc.ca

Provincial Archives of
Manitoba
200 Vaughan Street
Winnipeg, MB R3C 1T5
Reference: 204-945-3971
Fax: 204-948-2008
www.gov.mb.ca/chc/archives/
index.html

Provincial Archives of New
Brunswick
Dineen Drive, UNB Campus
Fredericton
mailing address: Box 6000
Fredericton, NB E3B 5H1
Tel: 506-453-2122
Fax: 506-453-3288
www.gov.nb.ca/supply/archives

Provincial Archives of
Newfoundland and Labrador
Colonial Building, Military
Road
St. John's, NL A1C 2C9
Tel: 709-729-3065
Fax: 709-729-0578
www.gov.nf.ca/panl/

Northwest Territories Archives
Prince of Wales Northern
Heritage Centre
Box 1320
Yellowknife, NT X1A 2L9
Tel: 867-873-7657
Fax: 867-873-0205
www.pwnhc.learnnet.nt.ca/
programs/archives.htm

Public Archives of Nova Scotia
6016 University Avenue
Halifax NS B3H 1W4
Tel: 902-424-6060
Fax: 902-424-0628
www.nsarm.ednet.ns.ca

Nunavut Archives
P.O. Box 310
Igloolik NV X0A 0L0
Tel: 867-934-8626
E-mail: eatkinson@gov.nv.ca
Public Archives of Nova Scotia
6016 University Avenue
Halifax, NS B3H 1W4
Tel: 902-424-6060
Fax: 902-424-0628
www.nsarm.ednet.ns.ca

Archives of Ontario
77 Grenville Street, Unit 300
Toronto, ON M5S 1B3
Tel: 416-327-1582
Fax: 416-327-1999
www.gov.on.ca/MCZCR/
archives

Public Archives and Records
Office of Prince Edward Island
4th floor, Hon. George Coles
Building,

Richmond Street,
Charlottetown
mailing address: Box 1000
Charlottetown, PE C1A 7M4
Tel: 902-368-4290
Fax: 902-368-6327
www2.gov.pe.ca/educ/archives

Direction des Archives
Nationales de l'Est du Québec
Pavillon Louis-Jacques Cassault
1210 avenue du Seminaire,
Sainte-Foy
mailing address: C.P. 10450
Sainte-Foy, QC G1V 4N1
Tel: 418-643-8904
Fax: 418-646-0868
www.anq.gouv.qc.ca

Direction des Archives
Nationales de l'Ouest du
Québec
535, avenue Viger est
Montréal, QC H2L 2P3
Tel: 514-873-6000
Fax: 514-873-2950
www.anq.gouv.qc.ca
[Presumably, either of these
central administrations will
direct your query to the
appropriate regional centre.]

Saskatchewan Archives Board
University of Saskatchewan, Rm 91
Murray Building
3 Campus Drive
Saskatoon, SK S7N 5A4
Tel: 306-933-5832
Fax: 306-933-7305
www.gov.sk.ca/govt/archives

Saskatchewan Archives Board
University of Regina
3737 Wascana Parkway
Regina, SK S4S 0A2
Tel: 306-787-4068
Fax: 306-787-1179
www.gov.sk.ca/govt/archives

Yukon Territory Archives
Box 2703, 400 College Drive
Whitehorse, YT Y1A 2C6
Tel: 867-667-5321
Fax: 867-393-6253
www.yukoncollege.yk.ca/archives/
yukarch.html

VITAL STATISTICS OFFICES

Since vital statistics [i.e. birth, marriage and death registrations] are under the jurisdiction of the provinces, there are no records at the federal level, but the latest addresses, etc., are available at the Archives Web site listed in *Tracing Your Ancestors*. Registration began at various times in the different provinces, but none are earlier than the 1860s.

PROVINCIAL OFFICES

Alberta Government Services
Registries Division
Box 2023
Edmonton, AB T5J 4W7
Tel: 780-427-2683
Fax: 780-422-4225
www.gov.ab.ca/ma

British Columbia
Vital Statistics Agency
818 Fort Street, Victoria
mailing address: Box 9657
Station Provincial
Government
Victoria, BC V8W 9P3
Tel: 250-952-2681
Fax: 250-952-2576
www.hlth.gov.bc.ca/vs/

Manitoba Consumer &
Corporate Affairs, Vital
Statistics
254 Portage Avenue
Winnipeg, MB R3C 0B6
Tel: 204-945-3701
Fax: 204-948-3128
www.gov.mb.ca

New Brunswick
Department of Health &
Community Services
Vital Statistics
Box 6000
Fredericton, NB E3B 5H1
Tel: 506-453-7411
Fax: 506-453-3245
www.gov.nb.ca/hcs-ssc

Newfoundland and
Labrador Department of
Government Services &
Lands Vital Statistics
Division
5 Mews Place, St. John's
mailing address: Box 8700
St. John's, NL A1B 4J6
Tel: 709-729-3311
Fax: 709-729-2071
www.gov.nf.ca/gsl/

Northwest Territories Dept. of
Health & Social Services
Vital Statistics
Bag 9
Inuvik, NT X0E 0T0
Tel: 867-777-7420
Fax: 867-777-3197
www.gov.nt.ca/

Nova Scotia Department of
Business & Commercial Services
Vital Statistics
Joseph Howe Building
1690 Hollis Street, Halifax
mailing address: Box 157
Halifax, NS B3J 2M9
Tel: 902-424-4381
Fax: 902-424-0678
www.gov.ns.ca/bacs/vstat

Ontario Minister of Consumer
& Commercial Relations
Registrar General Branch
189 Red River Road
Thunder Bay
mailing address, Box 4600
Thunder Bay, ON P7B 6L8
Tel: 1-800-461-2156
or: 416-325-8305
Fax: 807-343-7459
www.ccr.gov.on.ca/mccr

P.E.I. Department of Health
and Social Services, Vital
Statistics
Box 3000
Montague, PE C0A 1R0
Tel: 902-838-0882
Fax: 902-838-0883
www.gov.pe.ca/hss/index.html
[use "search" or F A Questions]

Province du Québec
Le Directeur de L'Etat Civil
Service à la clientele
205 rue Montmagny
Québec, QC G1N 2Z9
Tel: (Québec) 418-643-3900;
(Montréal) 514-864-3900
Elsewhere in Qué. 800-567-3900
Fax: 418-646-3255
www.etatcivil.gouv.qc.ca

Saskatchewan Health
Vital Statistics & Health
Insurance Registration Branch
1919 Rose Street
Regina, SK S4P 3V7
Tel: 306-787-1167
Fax: 306-787-8310
www.gov.sk.ca/govt/health

Yukon Health & Social Services
Vital Statistics
Box 2703
Whitehorse, YT Y1A 2C6
Tel: 867-667-5207
Fax: 867-393-3069
www.hss.gov.yk.ca/

GENEALOGICAL SOCIETIES

NATIONAL
Canadian Federation of
Genealogical & Family History
Societies (CANFED)
227 Parkville Bay
Winnipeg, MB R2M 2J6
Tel: 204-256-6176
The federation maintains no
library and no longer issues a
newsletter.

East European Genealogical
Society
Box 2536
Winnipeg, MB R3C 4A7
Tel: 204-989-3292
www.eegsociety.org
Maintains a library and issues a
journal: *East European Genealogist*

Huguenot Society of Canada
Ste 105, 4936 Yonge Street
Toronto, ON M2N 6S3
Tel: 416-222-1967
Publishes a newsletter: *Huguenot
Trails*

Jewish Genealogical Society
of Canada (JGS)
Box 446, Station A
Toronto, ON M2N 5T1
Maintains a library and issues a
journal: *Shem Tov*

Société généalogique canadienne-
française
3440, rue Davidson, Montréal
mailing address: C.P. 335, Station
Place d'Armes
Montréal, QC H2Y 3H1
Tel: 514-527-1010
Fax: 514-527-0265
www.sgcf.com/
Maintains a library and issues a
journal: *Memoires …*

Ukrainian Genealogical &
Historical Society of Canada
R.R. No.2
Cochrane, AB T0L 0W0
Telephone/Fax: 403-932-6811
feefhs.org/ca/frgughsc.html
Maintains a library and issues a
journal: *Nase Leude/Our People*

United Empire Loyalists'
Association of Canada (UEL)
Suite 202, George Brown
House
50 Baldwin Street
Toronto, ON M5T 1L4
Tel: 416-591-1783
Fax: 416-591-7506
www.npiec.on.ca/ uela/
uela1.htm
The UEL Association has a
number of branches across
Canada that are not listed
here; check the Web site.
Maintains a library and
issues a journal: *Loyalist
Gazette*

PROVINCIAL
Alberta Genealogical Society
(AGS)
Prince of Wales Armouries
Heritage Centre
#116 - 10440-108 Avenue
Edmonton, AB T5H 3Z9
Tel: 403-424-4429
Fax: 403-423-8980
www.compusmart.ab.ca/
abgensoc
Maintains a library and
issues a journal: *Relatively
Speaking*

The Alberta Genealogical
Society has branches
throughout the province that
are not listed here; check
the Web site. The Alberta
Family History Society is a
separate organization in
Calgary. It has no branches.

Alberta Family History Society (AFHS)
Box 30270, Station B
Calgary, AB T2M 4P1
Tel: 403-214-1447
www.afhs.ab.ca
Maintains a library and issues a journal: *Chinook*

British Columbia Genealogical Society (BCGS)
Box 88054, Lansdowne Mall
Richmond, BC V6X 3T6
Tel: (604-502-9119
Fax: 604-263-4952
www.npsnet.com/bcgs/
Maintains a library and issues a journal: *British Columbia Genealogist*
There are a number of individual local genealogical organizations throughout the province unaffiliated with the British Columbia Genealogical Society that are not listed here but are listed on the Veinot website. See p.82. The society in Victoria is the next largest genealogical society in the province.

Victoria Genealogical Society (VGS)
Box 45031, Mayfair Postal Outlet
Victoria, BC V8Z 7G9
Tel: 250-360-2808
www.islandnet.com/ vgs/ homepage.html
Maintains a library and issues a journal: *The Journal of the Victoria Genealogical Society*

Manitoba Genealogical Society (MGS)
Unit A, 1045 St James Street
Winnipeg, MB R3H 1B1
Tel: 204-783-9139
Fax: 204-783-0190
www.mbnet.mb.ca/ mgs
Maintains a library and issues a journal: *Generations*. The Manitoba Genealogical Society has branches throughout the province that are not listed here; check the Web site. There are a number of independent groups in the province as well.

New Brunswick Genealogical Society (NBGS)
Box 3235, Station B
Fredericton, NB E3A 5G9
Telephone/Fax: [none noted]
www.bitheads.ca/nbgs/
Maintains a library and issues a journal: *Generations*. The New Brunswick Genealogical Society is composed of representatives of each of its branches throughout the province that are not listed here. For further information, go to the NBGS Web site. As well, there are some independent groups in the province.

Centre d'études Acadiennes
Université de Moncton
Moncton, NB E1A 3E9
Tel: 506-858-4085
Fax: 506-858-4530
www.umoncton.ca/ etudeacadiennes/centre/ cea.html

Maintains a library and issues a journal: *Contact-Acadie*

Newfoundland & Labrador Genealogical Society, Inc. (NLGS)
Colonial Building, Military Road
St. John's, NL A1C 2C9
Tel: 709-754-9525
Fax: 709-754-6430
www3.nf.sympatico.ca/nlgs
Maintains a library and issues a journal: *The Newfoundland Ancestor*.

Northwest Territories Genealogical Society (NTGS)
Box 1715
Yellowknife, NT X1A 2P3
Tel: [none noted]
Fax: 867-873-9304
www.ssimicro.com/nonprofit/nwtgs/
Issues a journal: *Under the Jack Pine*

Genealogical Association of Nova Scotia (GANS)
Box 641, Station Central
Halifax, NS B3J 2T3
Tel: 902-454-0322
Fax: [none noted]
www.chebucto.ns.ca/Recreation/GANS/
Maintains a library and issues a journal: *The Nova Scotia Genealogist*. Nova Scotia has a number of individual genealogical societies unaffiliated with The Genealogical Association of Nova Scotia that are not listed here. Check the Veinot Web site noted on p.82.

Genealogical Institute of the Maritimes
P.O. Box 36022
Canada Post Postal Office
5675 Spring Garden Road
Halifax, NS B3J 1G0
nsgna.ednet.ns.ca
Publishes *East Coast Roots*

Ontario Genealogical Society (OGS)
102 - 40 Orchard View Blvd
Toronto, ON M4R 1B9
Tel: 416-489-0734
Fax: 416-489-9803
www.ogs.on.ca
Maintains a library and issues a journal: *Families*. The OGS has 30 branches throughout the province that are not listed here; check the Web site. As well, there are a number of genealogical organizations, unaffiliated with OGS, located throughout the province.

Société franco-ontarienne d'histoire et de généalogie
C.P. 8254 - Succursale T
Ottawa, ON K1G 3H7
Tel: 613-729-5769
Fax: [none noted]
laurentian.ca/sfohg
Maintains a library and issues a journal: *Le Chaînon*. The Société franco-ontarienne has many branches throughout Ontario; contact the provincial group for the address of the branch in your area of interest.

Prince Edward Island
Genealogical Society (PEIGS)
Box 2744
Charlottetown, PE C1A 8C4
Telephone/Fax: [none noted]
<www.islandregister.com/
peigs.html
Maintains a library and issues a
journal: *P.E.I. Genealogical
Society, Inc Newsletter*

The Province of Quebec has
the largest number of
individual genealogical groups,
most of which are affiliated
with the provincial federation.
They are not listed here
individually. The major
English and French-speaking
societies are listed below.

Fédération québecoise des
sociétés de généalogie
C.P. 9454
Sainte-Foy, QC G1V 4A8
Tel: 418-651-9127
Fax: 418-651-2643
www.federationgenealogie.qc.ca
Does not maintain a library but
issues a journal: *Info-Genealogie*

Quebec Family History Society
Box 1026
Pointe Claire, QC H9S 4H9
Tel: 514-695-1502
www.cam.org/~qfhs/index.html
[This is the English-speaking
society] Maintains a library and
issues a journal: *Connections*

Société de généalogie de Québec
C. P. 9066
Sainte-Foy, QC G1V 4A8
Tel: 418-651-9127
Fax: 418-651-2643
www.genealogie.org.club/sgq/
[This is the major French-
speaking society]
Maintains a library and issues a
journal: *L'ancêtre*

Société de généalogie de
l'Outaouais
C.P. 2025, Succursale B
Hull, QC J8X 3Z2
Tel: 819-772-3010
Fax: [none noted]
www3.sympatico.ca/sgo/
Maintains a library and issues a
journal: *L'Outaouais
Genealogique*

Saskatchewan Genealogical
Society (SGS)
2nd floor, 1870 Lorne Street,
Regina
mailing address: Box 1894
Regina, SK S4P 3E1
Tel: 306-780-9207
Fax: 306-781-6021
www.saskgenealogy.com/
Maintains a library and issues a
journal: *The Bulletin*. The
Saskatchewan Genealogical
Society has a number of
branches throughout the
province that are not listed here;
check the Web site.

Yukon Territory Genealogical Society at the Dawson City Museum and Historical Society
Box 303
Dawson City, YT Y0B 1G0
Tel: 867-993-5291

Fax: [none noted]
users.yknet.yk.ca/dcpages/ Museum.html
Maintains a library and issues a journal: *Dawson City Museum Newsletter*

LIBRARIES

Almost every town and city in Canada has a public library, or is part of a library network; every college and university in the country has a library, if not several. They all maintain excellent reference tools and most hold material relating to local families and local history. However, it is impossible to list all of them in these few pages.

One can assume that the main branch of the public library in every urban centre will have a good, and sometimes excellent, genealogical and local history collection, often housed in a special room. Some also hold the collections of the local genealogical or historical society. In addition, expect them to have a representative selection of local newspapers and serials and, possibly, maps.

For addresses and telephone numbers consult local telephone directories or whichever of those Canadian library directories a local library subscribes to. Four of these are *Canadian Almanac & Directory, 2000*, 153rd ed. (Toronto: Micromedia, annual); *Directory of Libraries in Canada/ Répertoire des bibliothèques du Canada* (Toronto: Micromedia, annual); *Directory of Special Collections of Research Value in Canadian Libraries/Répertoire des collections spécialisées dans les bibliothèques candiennes* (Ottawa, National Library of Canada, 1992); and one that contains special libraries and archives: the *Directory of Special Libraries in the Toronto Area*, 14th ed. (Toronto: S.L.A., Toronto Chapter, 1996). As well, for those of you on the Internet, check Library and Archives Canada's

Web site, which also maintains the names, street addresses and web addresses of all Canadian library organizations.

Library of Canada
395 Wellington Street
Ottawa, ON K1A 0N4
Tel: 613-995-9481
Fax: 613-943-1112
www.nlc-bnc.ca

PROVINCIAL LIBRARIES

ALBERTA
Calgary Public Library
W.R. Castell (Central) Library
Local History Collection
616 Macleod Trail S.E.
Calgary, AB T2G 2M2
Tel: 403-260-2785
Fax: 403-237-5393
calgarypubliclibrary.com/
library/genealogy.htm

Edmonton Public Library,
Main Br
7 Sir Winston Churchill
Square
Edmonton, AB T5J 2V4
Tel: 780-496-7020
Fax: 780-496-1885
www.publib.edmonton.ab.ca/

Glenbow Library and Archives
130-9th Avenue S.E.
Calgary, AB T2G 0P3
Tel: 403-268-4197
Fax: 403-232-6569
www.glenbow.org/

BRITISH COLUMBIA
Vancouver Public Library
Special Collections
350 West Georgia Street
Vancouver, BC V6B 6B1
Tel: 604-331-3603
Fax: 604-331-4080
www.vpl.ca/branches/
LibrarySquare/spe/
guidetosc.html

Greater Victoria Public Library
735 Broughton Street
Victoria, BC V8W 3H2
Tel: 250-382-7241
Fax: 250-382-7125
www.gvpl.ca/index.shtml

Surrey Centennial Library
Cloverdale Branch
5642 - 176A Street
Surrey, BC V3S 4G9
Tel: 604-576-1384
Fax: 604-576-0120
www.spl.surrey.bc.ca/
SearchtheWeb/Genealogy/
Default.htm

University of British Columbia
Special Collections
1956 Main Mall
Vancouver, BC V6T 1Z1
Tel: 604-822-3871
Fax: 604-822-3893
www.library.ubc.ca/

MANITOBA
Archives of Manitoba
254 Portage Avenue
Winnipeg, MB R3C 0B6
Tel: 204-945-3701
Fax: [not noted]
www.gov.mb.ca/chc/archives/
genealogy/gen_text/
outside_records.html

Manitoba Legislative Library
Main Reading Room
Main floor
200 Vaughan Street
Winnipeg, MB R3C 1T5
Tel: 204-945-4330
Fax: 204-948-1312
<www.gov.mb.ca/chc/leg-lib/
ll_heritage.html

Winnipeg Public Library
251 Donald Street
Winnipeg, MB R3C 3P5
Tel: 204-986-6450
Fax: 204-984-4072
wpl.winnipeg.ca/library/
contact/branches/
centennial.asp

NEW BRUNSWICK
University of New Brunswick
Harriet Irving Library
5 MacAulay Drive, Fredericton
mailing address: Box 7500
Fredericton, NB E3B 5H5
Tel: 506-453-3546
Fax: 506-453-4831

Harriet Irving Library Archives
and Special Collections
The Loyalist Collection
[address as above]
Tel: 506-453-4834
Fax: 506-453-4749
www.lib.unb.ca/collections/
loyalist

Mount Allison University
Ralph Pickard Bell Library
Archives Collection
49 York Street
Sackville, NB E4L 1C6
Tel: 506-364-2563
Fax: 506-364-2617
www.mta.ca/library/

L.P. Fisher Public Library
679 Main Street
Woodstock, NB E7M 2E1
Tel: 506-328-6880
Fax: 506-325-9527
www.gnb.ca/0003/
woodstock.html

Saint John Free Public Library
1 Market Square
Saint John, NB E2L 4Z6
Tel: 506-643-7220
Fax: 506-643-7225
www.sjfn.nb.ca/sjfn_sjrl.html

Moncton Public Library
644 Main Street, Suite 101
Moncton, NB E1C 1E2
Tel: 506-869-6000
Fax: 506-869-6022
www.moncton.org/search/
english/CITYLIVING/
yourleisure/library.htm

NEWFOUNDLAND AND LABRADOR
Provincial Reference &
Resource
Library, Newfoundland Section
Arts and Cultural Centre
125 Allandale Road
St. John's, NL A1B 3A3
Tel: 709-737-3955
Fax: 709-737-3009
www.publib.nf.ca/php/
libhours.php?lcode=sjh

Memorial University of
Newfoundland
Queen Elizabeth II Library
Centre for Newfoundland
Studies
General Delivery
St. John's, NL A1B 3Y1
Tel: 709-737-7475
Fax: 709-737-2153
www.library.mun.ca

Corner Brook Public Library
Box 2006
Corner Brook, NL A2H 6J8
Tel: 709-634-0013
Fax: 709-634-0330
hera.publib.nf.ca/php/
libhours.php?lcode=wcb

NORTHWEST TERRITORIES
Yellowknife Public Library
Centre Square Mall, 2nd fl
5022-49th Street, Yellowknife
mailing address: Box 694
Yellowknife, NT X1A 2N5
Tel: 867-920-5642
Fax: 867-920-5671
library@city.yellowknife.nt.ca

Prince of Wales Northern
Heritage Centre
Culture & Heritage Library
Government of the Northwest
Territories
Box 1320
Yellowknife, NT X1A 2L9
Tel: 867-873-7177
Fax: 867-873-0205
pwnhc.learnnet.nt.ca/

NOVA SCOTIA
University College of Cape
Breton
The Beaton Institute Archives
Box 5300
Sydney, NS B1P 6L2
Tel: 902-563-1329
Fax: 902-562-8899
beaton.uccb.ns.ca/home.htm

Acadia University
Vaughan Memorial Library
Planter Studies Centre
50 Acadia Street
Wolfville, NS B0P 1X0
Tel: 902-585-1505
Fax: 902-585-1070
library.acadiau.ca/archives/
hours.html

ONTARIO
North York Public Library
Gladys Allison Canadiana
Room
6th floor, 5120 Yonge Street
Toronto, ON M2N 5N9
Tel: 416-395-5623
Fax: 416-395-5668
www.tpl.toronto.on.ca/
uni_can_genealogy.jsp#society

Toronto Reference Library
Genealogy & History Section
4th floor, 789 Yonge Street
Toronto, ON M4W 2G8
Tel: 416-393-7155
Fax: 416-393-7229
www.tpl.toronto.on.ca/
uni_spe_genealogy.jsp

Hamilton Public Library
Special Collections
Box 2700, Stn LCD 1
Hamilton, ON L8N 4E4
Tel: 905-546-3408
Fax: 905-546-3203
www.hpl.Hamilton.on.ca

Kitchener Public Library
Gladys Schmidt Room of Local
History
85 Queen Street North
Kitchener, ON N2H 2H1
Tel: 519-743-0271
Fax: 519-570-1360
<www.kpl.org/fyi_geneal.shtml

London Public Library
Central Branch
251 Dundas Street
London, ON N6A 6H9
Tel: 519-661-4600
Fax: 519-663-5396
www.londonpubliclibrary.ca/
static/generic/89

Brock University
James A. Gibson Library
Special Collections
500 Glenridge Avenue
St Catharines, ON L2S 3A1
Tel: 905-688-5550 x 3264
Fax: 905-988-5490
www.brocku.ca/library/

Queen's University
Joseph S. Stauffer Library
Kingston, ON K7L 5C4
Tel: 613-545-2519
Fax: 613-545-6362
library.queensu.ca/stauffer/

Pickering College Carolyn
Sifton Library
Canadian Yearly Meeting
Archives
Dorland Friends [Quakers]
Historical Collection
16945 Bayview Avenue
Newmarket, ON L3Y 4X2
Tel: 905-895-1700 x328
Fax: 905-895-9076
www.pickeringcollege.on.ca/

PRINCE EDWARD ISLAND
Prince Edward Island Museum
and Heritage Foundation
2 Kent St.
Charlottetown, PE C1A 1M6
Tel: 902-368-6600
Fax: 902-368-6600
www.peimuseum.com/
index.html
peimuse@pei.sympatico.ca

QUEBEC
Bibliothèque de Montréal
Centrale
Collection Gagnon
1210 rue Sherbrooke est
Montréal, QC H2L 1L9
Tel: 514-872-1616
Fax: 514-872-4654
www2.ville.montreal.qc.ca/
biblio/pageacc.htm

City of Montréal Archives
275 Notre-Dame Est
Bureau S1.07
Montréal, QC H2Y 1C6
Tel: 514-872-2615
Fax: 514-872-3475
www2.ville.montreal.qc.ca/
archives/archives.htm

Bishop's University
Eastern Townships Research
Centre
Faculty Box 127
McGreer Hall
Lennoxville, QC J1M 1Z7
Tel: 819-822-9600 x2609
Fax: 819-822-9661
www.etrc.ca/archives.html

Musée McCord Museum
690 rue Sherbrooke ouest
Montréal, QC H3A 1E9
Tel: 514-397-7100
Fax: 514-398-5045
www.musee-mccord.qc.ca/

SASKATCHEWAN
Regina Public Library
Prairie History Room
Box 2311
Regina, SK S4P 3Z5
Tel: 306-777-6011
Fax: 306-352-5550
www.reginalibrary.ca/
index.cfm?page=30

Saskatoon Public Library
Frances Morrison Branch
Local History Room
311 - 23rd Street East
Saskatoon, SK S7K 0J6
Tel: 306-975-7578
Fax: 306-975-7542
www.publib.saskatoon.sk.ca/
morrison.html

Association of United
Ukrainian Canadians-
Saskatchewan, Library
1809 Toronto Street
Regina, SK S4P 1M7
Tel: 306-787-9520
Fax: 306-352-5543
www.auuc.org

YUKON
Dawson City Museum and
Historical Society Library
Box 303
Dawson City, YT Y0B 1G0
Ph.: 867-993 5291
Fax: 867-993 5839
users.yknet.yk.ca/dcpages/
Museum.html

A Framework of Useful Dates

1604, First formal attempt to colonize Acadia.

1710, 13 October, British capture Port Royal and rename it Annapolis Royal.

1713, 11 April, Treaty of Utrecht: British title to Newfoundland and mainland Nova Scotia established. France retains Île-Royale, Île St-Jean and lands north of Chignecto.

1745, 17 June, Louisbourg surrendered to British.

1748, 18 October, Treaty of Aix-la-Chapelle, Louisbourg returned to France.

1749, 9 July, Halifax founded.

1755, June, British capture French forts in Chignecto, begin expulsion of Acadians from Nova Scotia.

1758, 26 July, British recapture Louisbourg.

1759, 13 September, Battle of the Plains of Abraham at Quebec City.

1760, 8 September, Capitulation of Montreal, Canada surrendered to British.

1763, 10 February, Treaty of Paris ends Seven Years War. France cedes Canada and remaining colonies in Acadia to Great Britain.

7 October, Royal Proclamation of 1763 establishes boundaries and governments for new colonies, Canada renamed Province of Quebec.

1764, 10 August, establishment of civil government in Province of Quebec.

1774, 5 September, 1st Continental Congress meets at Philadelphia.

1775, September, American Army invades Quebec, takes Montreal, attacks Quebec city.

1778, 29 March, Capt. James Cook sights land at Vancouver Island.

1783, 3 September, Treaty of Paris (Treaty of Separation) by which Britain formally recognized the United States of America.

1784, November, New Brunswick and Cape Breton become separate colonies.

1791, 26 December, Canada or Constitutional Act (passed 10 June) comes into force. Province of Quebec split into Lower Canada and Upper Canada.

1792, Capt. George Vancouver enters Burrard inlet.

1794, 19 November, Jay's Treaty regulating commerce and navigation signed by United States and Britain.

1812, The Earl of Selkirk's Scottish settlers arrive at the junction of the Red and Assiniboine Rivers.

June, United States invades Upper Canada beginning the War of 1812, concluded by the Treaty of Ghent, 24 Dec. 1814.

1837–38, rebellions in Upper and Lower Canada.

1841, 10 February, Act of Union proclaimed, Upper and Lower Canada united as the Province of Canada, with a single legislature. Lower Canada (Quebec) termed Canada East, Upper Canada (Ontario), Canada West.

1849, 13 January, Hudson's Bay Co. granted 10-year trade monopoly on Vancouver Island and in exchange were to establish a colony there. The first governor of the colony arrived at Victoria in March 1850.

1858, 30 May, Hudson's Bay. Co. rights to Vancouver Island revoked.

1 July, first Canadian coins introduced: 1¢, 5¢, 10¢ 20¢

August, Colony of British Columbia (mainland) established.

1861, American Civil War or War Between the States begins (ended April 1865).

1866, Fenian Raids at Fort Erie (Canada West), Pigeon Hill (Canada East).

17 November, Colony of Vancouver Island annexed to British Columbia.

1867, 1 July, Confederation. British North America Act establishes the Dominion Of Canada with New Brunswick, Nova Scotia, Ontario and Quebec.

1870, 11 May, Dominion of Canada pays £300,000 for Rupert's Land (the provinces of Ontario and Quebec north of the Laurentians and West of Labrador; all of Manitoba; most of Saskatchewan; the southern half of Alberta; the eastern part of Nunavut Territory; and portions of Minnesota and North Dakota in the United States).

1870, 15 July, Manitoba made a province of Canada.

1871, 20 July, British Columbia joins Canada.

1873, 1 July, Prince Edward Island joins Canada.

1898, Yukon Act makes Yukon a separate Territory.

1905, Alberta and Saskatchewan become provinces of Canada.

1912, Northwest Territories boundaries adjusted to enlarge Ontario and Quebec.

1947, Canadian Citizenship Act comes into force.

1949, Newfoundland and Labrador join Confederation

1999, 1 April, Nunavut Territory comes into being.

2001, 6 December, Constitution Act amended to rename Province of Newfoundland the Province of Newfoundland and Labrador.

For fuller details of any event, consult The Fitzhenry & Whiteside *Book of Canadian Facts & Dates*, comp. Jay Myers, revised L. Hoffman and F. Sutherland (Richmond Hill, Ont.: Fitzhenry & Whiteside, 1991) and

Rupert's Land purchase: solon.org/Constitutions/Canada/English/rlo_1870.html

Newfoundland and Labrador name change: www.gg.ca/media/doc.asp?lang=e&DocID=1002

The Government of Nunavut: www.gov.nu.ca/

Ten Books That Are
Tools of the Trade

Bond, Mary E. *Canadian Directories, 1790-1987: a bibliography and place-name index*, 3 vols. Ottawa: National Library of Canada, 1989.

Harrison, Lorraine St-Louis and Mary Munk. *Tracing Your Ancestors in Canada*, Ottawa: National Archives of Canada, revised 2001. This may be obtained free by writing Library and Archives Canada, 395 Wellington St., Ottawa, ON Canada K1A 0N3 or downloaded from <www.archives.ca>.

Mann, Thomas. *The Oxford Guide to Library Research*, Oxford, New York: Oxford University Press, 1998.

Jetté, René. *Dictionnaire généalogique des familles du Québec*, Montreal: Les Presses de l'Université de Montréal, 1983.

Merriman, Brenda Dougall. *Genealogy in Ontario: Searching the Records*, Toronto: Ontario Genealogical Society (hereafter OGS), revised 3rd ed. 2002. Whichever British colony your ancestors may have settled in, the detailed descriptions of the typical colonial records generated in Ontario should prove helpful and useful.

Merriman, Brenda Dougall. *About Genealogical Standards of Evidence*, 2nd ed. Toronto: OGS, 2004. Updated and revised.

Mills, Elizabeth Shown. *Evidence! Citation & Analysis for the Family Historian*, Baltimore: Genealogical Publishing Company, 1997.

Punch, Terrence M. C.G.(C) with George F. Sanborne Jr. F.A.S.G. eds. *Genealogist's Handbook for Atlantic Canada Research*, Boston: New England Historic Genealogical Society, 2nd ed. 1997. Indispensable.

United Church of Canada, Committee on Archives and History, *Guide to Family History Research in the Archival Repositories of the United Church of Canada*, Toronto: OGS, 1996. In the process of being updated and revised.

Union List of Manuscripts in Canadian Repositories, Ottawa: Public Archives of Canada, 1975; Supplements (1979, 1982, c.1985). Continued on the Internet as Archives Canada <www.archivescanada.ca>.

Notes

These bibliographical notes give publication data on books and other publications, including CD-ROMs, mentioned in the text. Almost all are tools of the trade that you should know about, find and use.

Chapter One

1 T.R. Schellenberg, *Modern Archives Principles and Techniques* (Chicago: University of Chicago Press, 1956) p. 19.

2 Hilary Jenkinson, *The English Archivist: A New Profession*, 2nd ed. (London: H.K. Lewis, 1948), p. 4, as quoted in Schellenberg, p. 19.

3 Joyce Hemlow, with J.M.M.Burgess and A. Douglas, *A Catalogue of The Burney Family Correspondence 1749–1878* (New York, Montreal: New York Public Library, McGill University Press, 1971).

4 *Rules for Archival Description* (Ottawa: Bureau of Canadian Archivists, 1990).

5 F. Murray Greenwood and Barry Wright, eds., *Canadian State Trials* (Toronto: Published for the Osgood Society for Canadian Legal History by the University of Toronto Press, Vol.I, 1996, Vol.II, 2002). Both have an Appendix by Patricia Kennedy with very helpful advice to researchers.

6 For more information see Raymond Vézina, "Major Collections of Iconographic Works," *The Archivist*, vol. 7:2 (March–April, 1980), pp. 3–6.

Chapter Two

1 *Canadian State Trials*.

2 *Canadian State Trials*, vol. II, p. 408.

3 Althea Douglas and J. Creighton Douglas, *Canadian Railway Records: A Guide for Genealogists* (Toronto; OGS, 1994).

4 Phyllis, R. Blakeley, "Sir Samuel Cunard," *Dictionary of Canadian Biography, Vol. IX, 1861–1870* (Toronto: University of Toronto Press, 1976).

5 *Union List of Manuscripts in Canadian Repositories* (Ottawa: Public Archives of Canada, 1975) with *Supplements* (1979, 1982, c.1985).

6 *Canadian Periodical Index / Index de périodiques canadiens* (Toronto: Gale Canada, 1964–), an annual also published in monthly parts and available on computer laser optical disks since 1991.

Chapter Four

1 J. Brian Gilchrist and Clifford Duxbury Collier, comp., *Genealogy and Local History to 1900: a bibliography selected from the catalogue of the Canadian Institute for Historical Micro-reproductions (CIHM)/Généalogie et histoire locale d'avant 1900: une bibliographie tirée du catalogue de l'Institute canadien de microreproductions historiques (ICMH)* (Ottawa: CIHM-ICHM, 1995).

2 Danielle Lacasse and Antonio Lechasseur, *The National Archives of Canada 1872–1997*, Historical Booklet No. 58 (Ottawa: Canadian Historical Association, 1997) is a brief and informative history of the growth and development of the NAC.

3 Christopher Moore, *Louisbourg Portraits: Life in an Eighteenth-Century Garrison Town* (Toronto: Macmillan of Canada, 1982). See "A Note on the Sources," pp. 286–292.

Chapter Five

1 Noel M. Elliot, ed., *People of Ontario, 1600–1900: alphabetized directory of the people, places and vital dates*, 3 vol. (London, ON: Genealogical Research Library, 1984): *The French Canadians, 1600–1900: an alphabetized directory of the people, places, and vital dates*, 3 vol. (Toronto: Genealogical Research Library, 1992); *The Central Canadians, 1600–1900: an alphabetized directory of the people, places, and vital dates*, 3 vol. (Toronto: Genealogical Research Library, 1994); *The Atlantic Canadians, 1600–1900: an alphabetized directory of the people, places, and vital dates*, 3 vol. (Toronto: Genealogical Research Library, 1994); *The Western Canadians, 1600–1900: an alphabetized directory of the people, places, and vital dates*, 3 vol. (Toronto: Genealogical Research Library, 1994).

2 *Directories in Print*, 6th ed. (Detroit, Mich.: Gale Research Inc., c.1989– annual). For U.K. see also *BRAD Directories & Annuals* (London: Maclean Hunter Ltd., annual).

3 For other suggestions see *Oxford Guide to Library Research*, pp. 213–214.

4 Mary E. Bond, *Canadian Directories, 1790–1987: a bibliography and place-name index*, 3 vols. (Ottawa: National Library of Canada, 1989).

5 Dave Obee, comp., *Western Canadian Directories on microfiche and microfilm* (Victoria, BC: Dave Obee, 2003).

6 *The Eastern Townships Gazetteer and General Business Directory ... Containing Also Much Useful Information of a Miscellaneous Character* (St Johns/St Jean, Que.: Smith & Co., Proprietors of the "News", 1867). Reprinted by Page-Sangster Inc., 1967.

7 Terrence M. Punch C.G.(C), ed., *Genealogist's Handbook for Atlantic Canada Research*, with George F. Sanborne Jr., F.A.S.G., 2nd ed. (Boston: New England Historic Genealogical Society, 1997).

8 See *Tracing Your Ancestors in Canada*, pp. 27–28. Dave Obee's Back to the Land: A Genealogical Guide to Finding Farms on the Canadian Priaries (Victoria, BC: Dave Obee, 2001) contains an index to townships in the 1901 census.

9 *Répertoire alphabetique des mariages des Canadiens-français 1760–1935*, 49 vols. (Longueuil, QC: Services généalogiques Claude Drouin, ca. 1989–1990), and *Répertoire alphabetique des mariages des Canadiens-français 1760–1935: ordre féminin*, 64 vols. (Montreal: Institut généalogique Drouin, [1991?]).

10 *Répertoire des actes de baptême, mariage, sépulture et des recensements du Québec ancien*, ed Gaëtan Morin, vols. 1–30, 1621–1749, vols. 31–47, 1731–1765 (Montrèal: Universitè de Montréal, 1980–1991), now available on CD-ROM. A second CD-ROM contains the records for 1766–1799 (unpublished). The Indexes can be consulted on the Internet, where those who pay a subscription fee can also access the full database.

11 Compiled by the Prince Edward Island Museum and Heritage Foundation and the Genealogical Society, the *Master Name Index* and all genealogical services have been transferred to the Public Archives and Records Office, P.O. Box 1000, Charlottetown, PEI, C1A 7M4 Canada.

12 Edgar Ronald Seary, assisted by Sheila M.P. Lynch, *Family Names of the Island of Newfoundland*, new edition, corrected/edited by William J. Kerwin (St. John's: J.R. Smallwood Centre for Newfoundland Studies, Memorial University of Newfoundland, co-published with McGill-Queen's University Press, [1998]).

13 Stephen A. White, completing research by Hector-J. Hebert and Patrice Gallant, *Dictionnaire généalogique des familles acadiennes*, 2 vols. (Moncton, NB: Centre d'études acadiennes, Université de Moncton, 1999).

14 *Anglo-Celtic Roots: BIFHSGO Quarterly Chronicle*, vol. 8:2 (Spring 2002), p. ii. This issue also includes John Sayers's article, "Home Children," pp. 29–32.

15 *The Beaver* vol.82:2 (April/May 2002) pp. 14–21.

Chapter Six

1 René Jetté, *Dictionnaire généalogique des familles du Québec* (Montreal: Les Presses de l'Université de Montréal, 1983). Earlier, these returns were annotated and published by André Lafontaine: *Recensements annotés de la Nouvelle-France 1666 & 1667* and *Recensements annotés de la Nouvelle France 1681* (Sherbrooke, QC: A. Lafontaine, 1981 & 1985).

2 *1848 and 1850 Canada West (Ontario) Census Index: An Every-Name Index*, compiled by Brian Lee Dilts (Salt Lake City: Index Pub., 1984).

3 *Catalogue of Census Returns on Microfilm, 1666–1891*, comp. Thomas A. Hillman (Ottawa: Public Archives of Canada, 1987).

4 *Catalogue of Census Returns on Microfilm, 1901*, compiled by Thomas A. Hillman (Ottawa: National Archives of Canada, 1993).

5 Bruce S. Elliott, Dan Walker and Fawne Stratford-Devai, eds., *Men of Upper Canada: Militia Nominal Rolls, 1828–1829* (Toronto: OGS, 1995).

6 "Using Ships' Passenger Lists...", *Anglo-Celtic Roots*, vol.8:2 (Spring 2002), pp.48–51.

Chapter Seven

1   George Maclean Rose ed., *A Cyclopaedia of Canadian Biography being Chiefly Men of the Times* (Toronto: Rose Publishing Company, 1888); or see also *The Canadian Biographical Dictionary and Portrait Gallery of Eminent and Self-made Men: Ontario Volume* (Toronto, Chicago and New York: The American Biographical Publishing Company, 1880).

2   *Prominent People of the Maritime Provinces in Business and Professional Life* (Montreal, St. John, Vancouver: Canadian Publicity Co., 1922, 2nd. ed. 1938).

3   *Historical Atlas of Quebec Eastern Townships/Illustrated Atlas of the Eastern Townships and South Western Quebec* (Toronto: H. Belden & Co. 1881); reprint edition edited by Ross Cumming (Port Elgin: Ross Cumming, 1972).

4   Erastus G. Pierce, ed., *Men of Today in the Eastern Townships 1917*, intro. V.E.Morrill (Sherbrooke, QC: Sherbrooke Record Co., 1917).

5   *The Social Register of Canada*, 3 editions (Montreal: The Social Register of Canada, 1958–1961).

6   Leonard S. Channell, *History of Compton County and Sketches of the Eastern Townships, District of St. Francis and Sherbrooke County* (Cookshire Que.: L.S. Channell, 1896; Milton, Ont: Canadiana Reprint Series, No. 8, Global Heritage Press, 1999).

7   William F.F. Morley, *Ontario and the Canadian North. Vol.3: Canadian local histories to 1950: a bibliography* (Toronto: University of Toronto Press, c 1978).

8   Barbara B. Aitken, *Local Histories of Ontario Municipalities, 1951–1977: a bibliography* (Toronto: Ontario Library Association, 1978); with supplements covering ..., *1977–1987* (Toronto: Ontario Library Association, 1989); ..., *1987–1997* (Toronto: Ontario Genealogical Society, 1999).

9   Betty May, Frank McGuire and Heather Maddick, *County Atlases of Canada: a Descriptive Catalogue*, (Ottawa: National Map Collection, Public Archives of Canada, 1970).

10 Heather Maddick, comp., *County Maps: Land Ownership Maps of*

Canada in the 19th Century (Ottawa: National Map Collection, Public Archives of Canada, 1976).

Chapter Eight

1 Althea Douglas, *Here Be Dragons!* (Toronto: OGS, 1996), p. 35

2 Phillip G.A. Griffin-Allwood, "The Mystery of Baptist Records, or the Lack Thereof," *Generations* vol. 19:2 (NBGS: Summer 1996), pp. 32–36.

3 Glen Eker, *Jews Resident in Ontario According to the 1851 to 1901 Censuses of Canada* (Toronto: OGS, 2002).

4 See United Church of Canada Archives, *Guide to Research in the United Church of Canada Archives* (Toronto: OGS, 1996).

5 Canadian Friends Historical Association, *Genealogical Index to the Records of the Canadian Yearly Meeting of the Religious Society of Friends (Quakers), Volume I: Yonge Street Monthly Meeting.* (Newmarket, ON: Canadian Friends Historical Association, c1988).

Chapter Nine

1 *Directory of the Cemeteries in the Municipality of Metropolitan Toronto and Regional Municipality of York* (Toronto: Toronto Branch OGS, 1989).

2 William Inglis Morse, *Gravestones of Acadie* (London, A. Smith & Co., 1929) and *The Land of the New Adventure: The Georgian Era in Nova Scotia* (London, Bernard Quaritch Ltd., 1932).

3 Deborah Trask, *Life how short Eternity how long — Gravestone Carving and Carvers in Nova Scotia* (Halifax NS: Nova Scotia Museum, 1978).

4 Dorothy Relyea, comp., *Burial Records of Beechwood Cemetery 1873–1900* (Ottawa: Ottawa Branch OGS, 1991), *Beechwood Cemetery Interment Registry Index 1901–1930*, and … *1931–1955* (Ottawa: Ottawa Branch OGS, 1992, 1995). The CD title is *Beechwood Cemetery, Ottawa, Ontario* (Ottawa, c2000, 1 computer optical disc).

Chapter Ten

1 *The Beaver*, vol. 77:4 (August/September 1997), pp. 19–26.

2 Kathleen Jenkins, *Montreal: Island City of the St. Lawrence* (New York: Doubleday & Co. Inc., 1966), p. 284.

3 *The Beaver*, vol. 77:4 (August/September 1997), pp. 35–37.

4 W. Stewart Wallace, ed., "Journalism" *The Encyclopedia of Canada* Vol. III (Toronto: University Associates of Canada, 6 vols. 1940).

5 *Union List of Newspapers Held by Canadian Libraries* (1977 or 1983).

6 *Canadian Newspapers on Microfilm* (Ottawa: Canadian Library Association, 1959).

7 J. Brian Gilchrist, comp., *Inventory of Ontario Newspapers 1793–1986* (Toronto: Micromedia Ltd., 1987).

8 André Beaulieu and Jean Hamelin, *La presse Québecoise: des origines à nos jours. Index cumulatife*, 10 volumes, (Quebec: Université de Laval, 1973–1990).

9 "Journalism," pp. 310–315.

10 Gordon Ripley, ed., *Canadian Serials Directory* (Toronto: Reference Press, 1987).

11 *Matthews' List* (Meaford, ON: Syd Matthews & Partners, 199–?). Also known as *Matthews Media Directory*.

12 Sandra Burrows and Franceen Gaudet, *Checklist of Indexes to Canadian Newspapers* (Ottawa: National Library of Canada, 1987).

13 Daniel F. Johnson, B.B.A., C.G.(C) *Vital Statistics from New Brunswick (Canada) Newspapers* (Saint John, NB: D.F. Johnson, vol. 94, 2003). Prices and handling charges vary, write for an up to date price list. Address: Box 26025 Saint John, NB Canada E2J 4M3.

14 Some publications of Hunterdon House: Thomas B.Wilson, comp., *Ontario Marriage Notices*, (1982); D.A. McKenzie, comp., *Death Notices from the Christian Guardian 1836–1850*; also *1851–1860*, and *Obituaries from Ontario's Christian Guardian, 1861–1870* (1982, 1984, 1988), D.A. McKenzie, comp., *More Notices from Methodist Newspapers 1830–1857* (1986). *Ontario Register*, 8 vols. to date.

15 Marlene Simmons, *Index to Richford Vermont Gazette & Journal Gazette, 1880–1957: extracts of Canadian genealogical information* (Pointe Claire, Que: Quebec Family History Society, c1994).

Chapter Eleven

1 See *Here be Dragons!* "Geography ... for Genealogists" pp. 65–68. An expanded version can be found in "Geography, Genealogy and Railroads," Part I and Part II, *Families* vol. 34:2 & 3, May and Aug 1995.

2 *Historical Atlas of Canada*, 3 volumes (Toronto, Buffalo, London: University of Toronto Press). *Volume I*, edited by R. Cole Harris (1987); *Volume II*, edited by R. Louis Gentilcore, *et al.* (1993); *Volume III*, edited by Donald Kerr (1990). Designer/cartographer Geoffrey J. Matthews for all 3 volumes.

3 William G. Dean, et al., ed. *Concise Historical Atlas of Canada*, cartography by Geoffrey J. Matthew and Byron Moldofsky (Toronto, Buffalo, London: University of Toronto Press, 1998).

4 Christopher Andreae, *Lines of Country: An Atlas of Railway and Waterway History in Canada*, with cartography by Geoffrey Matthews (Erin, ON: Boston Mills Press, 1997).

Chapter Twelve

1 Sean Geer, *Pocket Internet* (London: Profile Books Ltd., in association with *The Economist* Newspaper Ltd., 2000), p.171.

Index

Other fine books by Althea Douglas

Canadian Railway Records
Althea and Creighton Douglas
Aids genealogists and family historians seek out the lists of companies, libraries, museums, archives and historical societies to find records of ancestors who worked with or for the railways.
1994 64p 1-55116-923-0 **$9.50**

Help I've Inherited an Attic Full of History second revised edition
"What do I do with all this stuff?" is the plea of those who find themselves the custodians of a portion of history. Included are simple conservation procedures, and extensive "not-before" lists to help date the objects.
2003 184p 0-7779-2129-4 **$33.00**

The Family Treasures Book
The 40th Anniversary Keepsake Project
Use this handy treasure book to keep track of your treasures
2001 40p 0-7779-2123-5 **$7.00/$2.00** with the purchase of Help! I've Inherited an Attic Full of History

Here be Dragons! Navigating the Hazards Found in Canadian Family Research
Researchers are aided with advice on changing social customs, common knowledge that is now forgotten, migration patterns and the splits and mergers that formed today's religious denominations.
1996 74p 0-7779-0196-X **$14.00**

Here be Dragons, Too! More Navigational Hazards for the Canadian Family Researcher
Moves beyond standard genealogical sources to examine other records. Includes advice on privacy and on computer research.
2000 88p 0-7779-0224-9 **$14.00**

More Tools of the Trade from the OGS

About Genealogical Standards of Evidence second edition
Brenda Dougall Merriman
How to properly document your research.
2004 0-7779-2135-9 **$16.00**

Genealogy in Ontario: Researching the Records revised third edition
Brenda Dougall Merriman
A must-have book for anyone with Ontario roots!
2002 278p 0-7779-2127-8 **$37.00**

The Genealogist's Journal
Susan Smart
Handy record book with hints to help your research and space for your valuable notes.
2003 112 p wiro binding hard card backing 0-7779-2130-8 **$14.95**